Author
FINISHER

THIS BOOK IS A **GIFT**

FROM

Jackie

FOR

Katie

ON

February 2022

BECAUSE

You are not alone.

Isaiah 41:10

NAME

A 365 Day Devotional to Frame Your Day

THE

With Positive Affirmations and Encouragement

DAY

WENDY K. WALTERS

Published in Corinth, Texas, by Palm Tree Publications. A division of Palm Tree Productions. www.palmtreeproductions.com

ISBN (hardcover): 978-0-9862033-7-4

ISBN (paperback): 978-0-9862033-8-1

TO CONTACT THE AUTHOR:

www.wendykwalters.com

Printed in the U.S.A.

SCRIPTURE VERSIONS USED IN THIS DEVOTIONAL

WHY NAME YOUR DAY?

When you name your day, you frame it. If I told you to keep your eyes open for a white truck today, you would notice them all day long. You would see white trucks everywhere. There wouldn't suddenly be an influx of white trucks on your commute, but because you spoke the words "white trucks," your brain would go to work looking for them. They were always there, but you didn't notice them until you heightened your awareness to see them.

When you name your day, you do the same thing. If I name my day POSSIBILITIES, I set my mind and spirit to become aware of possibilities that present themselves throughout the day. By decreeing that opportunities are present in the great moments and in trials, I open myself up to notice them. I ask God to help me become mindful and prepared to embrace them because I have framed my day with POSSIBILITIES.

I have been naming my day for several years and began sharing this concept with others. When I posted them on social media, there was an overwhelming, positive response. I have received so many testimonies of how God worked through naming the day that I started collecting the entries in a file. What you hold in your hands is the result.

Naming things is important. It was the first job God gave to Adam in the Garden. *"So the Lord God formed from the ground all the wild animals and all the birds of the sky. He brought them to man to see what he would call them, and the man chose a name for each one"* (Genesis 2:19, NLT). God created the animals, but He gave Adam dominion over them. God gave Adam the responsibility to name them, and in assigning their names, Adam stepped into his God-given authority. He entered into partnership with God.

Often, when someone's destiny began to activate, or a new and significant transition occurred in their life, God gave them a new name. Abram became Abraham. Sarai became Sarah. Jacob became Israel. Saul became Paul. At times, God instructed a name to be given from the start. It was God who named Adam. He named Isaac, Ishmael, and a few other Old Testament characters. Each name carried significant meaning, and when it was spoken aloud, it reverberated in agreement with God's covenant promise over that person. You may remember it was God who named John the Baptist ... and Jesus!

Often, our day takes us along with it. We react and respond to what presents itself: people, attitudes, tasks, schedules, responsibilities, etc. By day's end, we have grown tired and are often thankful just that we made it through. The Bible tells us, *"You will also declare a thing, and it will be established for you; so light will shine on your ways"* (Job 22:28, NKJV). By naming your day, you set the tone and establish what that day will bring to you. You put your mind and your spirit on the alert and begin to attract to you that which you have declared.

Words shape worlds. They have enormous creative power and potential. I invite you into a new realm of understanding and authority. I invite you to take dominion over your days by framing them with good things. Use this devotional to help you until the practice of naming your day has become a habit for you. In time, as you arise in the morning, what you should name your day will stir in your spirit, and as you come into agreement with what you declare, amazing things will happen!

May this be your best year yet,

Wendy

JANUARY

*Watch closely: I am preparing something new;
it's happening now, even as I speak,
and you're about to see it.
I am preparing a way through the desert;
waters will flow where there had been none.*

ISAIAH 43:19, VOICE

JANUARY 1

EXPANSION

God Himself will fill you with more.
Blessings upon blessings will be heaped upon you
and upon your children from the
maker of heaven and earth,
the very God who made you!

PSALM 115:14-15, TPT

I name this day EXPANSION. May the capacity of my soul become enlarged to receive more of God! I make room in my head and my heart for more—more of you, God—more healing, more restoration, more growth, more glory.

Today I welcome the stretching required to expand. Instead of complaining, I will rejoice, knowing this is part of Your plan for my EXPANSION!

What is an area where you feel like you are being stretched? Can you see how God is using this to expand you and fill you with more? Give yourself to the process of growth. Embrace the expansion with a glad and grateful heart.

2

IN SYNC

There is a time for everything,
and a season for every activity under the heavens.

ECCLESIASTES 3:1, NIV

I name this day IN SYNC. God has my past, my present, and my future in His hands. When I cooperate with Him, He orchestrates the most amazing things for me. He lines up people for me to meet, opportunities to share His love and wisdom, connections for business, and moments of joy and inspiration. It's beautiful!

When I try to push heaven around and set my plans without checking in first, I fumble all over the place. I know when I am out of sync, and I feel as effective as a fish flopping around away from the water where it was created to live, move, and have its being.

So, today I trust You, Lord. Help me to engage with all the people and places that keep me in time with the rhythm of heaven. Let me be so in tune with You that my instincts are spot on. Here's my hand, take it. Hold tightly, so it can't slip out easily. Let me feel Your grip. I trust Your path is just so much better than mine. Let's walk together today IN SYNC.

Even though the world is wrapped in darkness, God has bathed you in the glorious light of His glory! Let your heart arise, sing and rejoice in reverent jubilee. Stop now and pray. Seek God for how you can get in sync with heaven's rhythm today.

I BELONG

"Take this most seriously: A yes on earth is yes in heaven; a no on earth is no in heaven. What you say to one another is eternal. I mean this. When two of you get together on anything at all on earth and make a prayer of it, my Father in heaven goes into action. And when two or three of you are together because of me, you can be sure that I'll be there."

MATTHEW 8:18-20, MSG

I name this day I BELONG. I am stronger when I am connected with others. I am not a lone wolf, I am part of a team and I celebrate the success of everyone on my team.

Two heads are better than one, they have a greater return on their labor. "A cord of three strands is not easily broken."

I seek connectivity today. I will reach out to others. I will trust God to guide me to my team—my family, my tribe—and to protect me from linking with the wrong people. I am on an active search to plug in with those of like nature and ability. I am connected, I BELONG!

Who makes up the relationships that matter to you? With whom are you meaningfully connected to "do life" with together? Who values you and adds value to you? Be intentional today to connect with others.

FIRMLY ESTABLISHED

*I pray that my ways may become firmly
established so that I can obey Your laws.
Then I will never feel ashamed when I
study all your commandments.
I will give thanks to You as I learn Your regulations,
which are based on Your righteousness.
I will obey your laws. Never abandon me..*

PSALM 119:5-8, MSG

I name this day FIRMLY ESTABLISHED. May I follow Your course with steady steps; hearing and doing what You tell me.

My habits are powerful; they are the muscle memory of my will. I don't want any regrets, so I'll gladly embrace Your counsel. I see clearly the benefits in developing a pattern of righteous ways. In the safety of Your commandments, I am FIRMLY ESTABLISHED.

We all wobble when we walk at times. Our steps become steady when we are confident in our course with a clear path ahead. Where do you feel wobbly and in need of God's steadying counsel to firmly establish you?

VALIANT

*With God we shall do valiantly; it is He
who will tread down our foes.*

PSALM 60:12, ESV

I name this day VALIANT. With God's help I can do mighty things. I can perform with valor and gain the victory because it is He who tramples my enemies.

I am an overcomer. I am more than a conqueror. I am a valiant warrior and can do exploits. I am mighty through God. I pull down strongholds.

No matter my circumstances or how cowardly and trodden down I feel, I know victory is mine through Jesus. My feelings lie. God's truth is constant. Never in my strength, but always by God's power I am VALIANT.

VALIANT: *bravely determined, especially when
things are difficult, possessing or showing courage.*

When situations are challenging and hope is in short supply, that is when we need God's courage poured into us to be able to stand. As an act of faith, stand to your feet right now, place your hands on your hips in a power stance, imagine a cape flapping in the wind, and say, "I am a valiant warrior. I do exploits!"

ADVENTURE

"Come with me. I'll make a new kind of fisherman out of you. I'll show you how to catch men and women instead of perch and bass." They didn't ask questions, but simply dropped their nets and followed.

MATTHEW 4:19-20, MSG

I name this day ADVENTURE. God, I will follow you anywhere. Wherever it is you want me to go—I'll go!

Let's have an adventure together today, God. Let's see what trouble we can make for the enemy. Let's plunder hell and rescue souls out of the pit.

You make me brave. You make me fearless. My passion for You causes me to flee comfort and seek possibilities to make Your name great. Show me something I have never seen before. Today is a grand opportunity for an ADVENTURE!

When was the last time you felt truly adventurous? Let your inner child come out and play a little today. Be curious. Ask God to show you something new that inspires and delights you. Seize the day!

WHISPER

*Then he was told, "Go, stand on the mountain
at attention before God. God will pass by."
A hurricane wind ripped through the mountains
and shattered the rocks before God, but God
wasn't to be found in the wind; after the wind an
earthquake, but God wasn't in the earthquake; and
after the earthquake fire, but God wasn't in the fire;
and after the fire a gentle and quiet whisper.*

1 KINGS 19:11-12, MSG

I name this day WHISPER. I am keenly aware that You speak to me in a still, small voice. You whisper in my ear, gently directing my steps whenever I allow You to guide me. You whisper my name on the wind.

I will listen to the whisper. I will respond when You prompt. I won't second guess or be afraid, I will answer the call. You see. You know. You care. I trust Your voice. Today, I listen for Your WHISPER.

Quiet yourself and turn down the ambient noise. He is nearer than you can imagine, close enough to sense His heartbeat. Can you hear His whisper? What did He say?

SURROUNDED

*Therefore, since we are surrounded by such a great cloud
of witnesses, let us throw off everything that hinders
and the sin that so easily entangles. And let us run with
perseverance the race marked out for us, fixing our eyes
on Jesus, the pioneer and perfecter of faith. For the joy
set before Him He endured the cross, scorning its shame,
and sat down at the right hand of the throne of God.*

HEBREWS 12:1-2, NIV

I name this day SURROUNDED. Today I will remember that I am surrounded by a great cloud of witnesses; I am not alone. I feel the strength of their faith around me, cheering me on.

I humbly acknowledge my place in the great cloud and feel the weight of what they have carried before me. I feel God's love encircling me. I feel His grace on all sides. I am covered and completed because I am SURROUNDED.

Sometimes you feel alone, running your race in solitude. God promises not only that He is with you, but that He has you surrounded by a cheering cloud of witness!

RENOVATE

*Then Jesus said, "The Sabbath was made to serve
us; we weren't made to serve the Sabbath ..."*

MARK 2:28, MSG

I name this day RENOVATE. The sabbath was made for me (not me for it). It isn't some religious rule I keep, but a God-given, divine strategy for my good. He established the principle of rest at creation and continued it through the sabbath. I embrace His grace to be restored.

Today I declare a reset of my mind, will, and intellect. I plug into praise, so my spirit will be renewed. I take in the Word so my soul will be refreshed. I am grateful that God desires me to be refilled, revived, and recharged. I submit and graciously accept His call to RENOVATE.

RENOVATE: *to restore, refresh, replenish,
revive, fill up, return to original state.*

Is it hard for you to rest? Do you feel guilty about things left undone, pressured to perform them? How can you practically activate the principle of rest in your life?

CHOOSE

My counsel is this: Live freely, animated and motivated by God's Spirit. Then you won't feed the compulsions of selfishness. For there is a root of sinful self-interest in us that is at odds with a free spirit, just as the free spirit is incompatible with selfishness. These two ways of life are contrary to each other, so that you cannot live at times one way and at times another way according to how you feel on any given day. Why don't you choose to be led by the Spirit and so escape the erratic compulsions of a law-dominated existence?

GALATIANS 5:16-18, MSG

I name this day CHOOSE. I will exercise the free will God gave me to embrace His desires for me. I choose to walk by the Spirit. God's Spirit makes me free. I escape the law, sin, and death. I am released from the prison of selfishness and become animated by the Spirit of God alive and unfettered in me.

This is the day that the Lord has made, I choose to rejoice and be glad in it! I choose awesome. I choose hope. I choose happy. I have been chosen, therefore, with gratitude and joy, I CHOOSE!

Do you choose, or do you allow people and circumstances to force you to a place where you feel, "I had no choice"? This always leads to regret. Where do you need to choose to be led by God's Spirit?

CELEBRATE

On your feet now—applaud God!
Bring a gift of laughter, sing yourselves into His presence.

PSALM 100:1-2, MSG

I name this day CELEBRATE. I will pull out every blessing and give myself over to active joy. I will delight in fulfilled promises, goals met, and dreams yet to reach for.

I exhibit jubilation! I will honor God with my laughter, with songs, yes, even with dancing! I will bring the party with me everywhere I go.

I am light, and today I choose to be colorful and bright light. May I breathe joy to heavy hearts and stoke the warm fires of gratitude in hearts which need a spark. Today, I CELEBRATE!

CELEBRATE: to actively confront negativity by
elevating every blessing; to visibly demonstrate
your gratitude with joy.

What can you celebrate today? What song just leapt into your heart right now? Sing it! Get alone in your car and shout, "Hallelujah!" Laugh and be glad!

FREEDOM FROM DISAPPOINTMENTS

*I will walk about in freedom, for I have
sought out Your precepts.*

PSALM 119:45, NIV

I name this day FREEDOM FROM DISAPPOINTMENTS. I have been let down—let down by leaders, by mentors, even by family and friends. They fell in front of me, mishandled my trust, led me to wrong places. They failed to nurture, failed to protect, some even left when I needed them most.

Today, I declare a release from the pain of disappointment, the heaviness of grief, and the damage of unmet expectations. By the power of the Spirit, I remove stumbling blocks left behind and I cancel stunted growth. Father, break the power and repetition of toxic patterns.

I am free today. I embrace the freedom. I will become the leader I longed for. I will mentor others in the way I desire to be mentored. Cherish, nurture, build, guard, propel—let that become my legacy. I speak FREEDOM FROM DISAPPOINTMENTS over myself today! Amen.

What has left you bogged down with disappointment lately? What has held you back from stepping into freedom from it? Don't wait another second. Take that first step toward releasing your pain and walking in your freedom today!

FRUITFUL

So as to walk in a manner worthy of the Lord,
fully pleasing to Him: bearing fruit in every good
work and increasing in the knowledge of God.

COLOSSIANS 1:10, ESV

I name this day FRUITFUL. I abide in the vine, therefore I bear much fruit.

God blesses the work of my hands. He causes increase. I sow in the morning and I sow again in the evening because I do not know whether one or both will produce fruit. As I walk worthy of God and please Him, I fulfill His covenant to multiply.

I trust in the Lord. I am like a tree planted by water, and my roots go down deep. I don't fall apart in trouble or wither in drought; whatever season I am in, I am FRUITFUL.

What bears fruit in your life? What grows weeds and thorns? Repentance pulls the weeds. Trusting and abiding in the Lord plants the seeds for abundant fruitfulness.

SET UP

As Peter, puzzled, sat there trying to figure out what
it all meant, the men sent by Cornelius showed up at
Simon's front door. They called in, asking if there was
a Simon, also called Peter, staying there. Peter, lost
in thought, didn't hear them, so the Spirit whispered
to him, "Three men are knocking at the door looking
for you. Get down there and go with them. Don't
ask any questions. I sent them to get you."

ACTS 10:20, MSG

I name this day SET UP. God has scheduled my divine connections for His greater purpose. I don't have to struggle or manipulate in order to gain opportunities.

I can trust God's voice, I need not doubt when He speaks. Like Cornelius sending for Peter, God will send me those who need what I've got. When they present themselves, I will know.

Today, I purposefully establish my awareness and carefully guard my conversations and thoughts. I will value every vessel I encounter and be on the alert for divine appointments. I have been SET UP!

Do you sometimes feel no one notices your growth or your gifts? It is tempting to manipulate notice. Can you trust that God will bring you opportunities in His time?

ABUNDANCE

God can pour on the blessings in astonishing ways so that you're ready for anything and everything, more than just ready to do what needs to be done.

2 CORINTHIANS 9:8, MSG

I name this day ABUNDANCE. I reject poverty's hold on my mind. I have been given the power to create wealth in order to establish God's covenant. I trust Him and obey His voice.

I name my seed just as I name my day. I expect a harvest—a return on investment. I know that in all labor there is profit and He blesses the work of my hands. I ask for increase today.

God has poured blessings on me in astonishing ways. This allows me to be a blessing in ways I have not before imagined. This joy of receiving and giving causes me to embrace ABUNDANCE.

LACK: *What I have can be taken away there will never be enough.*

ABUNDANCE: *What I have can always multiply, God has a never ending supply!*

Do you feel like God blesses you in astonishing ways or does the fear of lack disturb your trust and challenge your generosity? In what ways can you count your blessings? Determine today to shift your mind (and conversation) from lack to abundance.

RESOLUTE

*But Daniel resolved that he would not defile
himself with the king's food, or with the wine that
he drank. Therefore, he asked the chief of the
eunuchs to allow him not to defile himself.*

DANIEL 1:8, ESV

I name this day RESOLUTE. All my choices will be admirably purposeful. I desire to please God, unwavering in my faith, unswerving in my call. I am determined.

My actions spring forth from the words I speak, so I will carefully guard my thoughts and filter all my words through faith, examined by truth. I will agree with God. I am RESOLUTE.

RESOLUTE: *to be admirably purposeful,
determined, and unwavering.*

Can you identify an area of challenge where you need to strengthen your resolve to do it God's way? What truth from the Word will serve you in your resolve?

FUNDAMENTAL

Therefore thus says the Lord God, "Behold, I am the
one who has laid as a foundation in Zion, a stone,
a tested stone, a precious cornerstone, of a sure
foundation: 'Whoever believes will not be in haste.'"

ISAIAH 28:16, ESV

I name this day FUNDAMENTAL. My Lord, I have need of Thee. I stand on fundamental truths. I remember foundational teachings. They anchor me as I face things which challenge my faith and stretch me into higher, deeper, and wider experiences.

The odds are in my favor as one can chase a thousand and two can chase ten thousand. With You, nothing is impossible. You are my cornerstone. God, set my feet upon the Rock; keep me rooted and grounded in love. I will trust in You and cherish Your words to me. Willingly I embrace Your covenant. Acceptance of Your character and nature is to my faith, FUNDAMENTAL.

Do you need to revisit the foundational teachings of the faith? The bedrock of your belief provides solid footing upon which to stand. Where do you need confirmation?

REFUGE

God, You're such a safe and powerful place to find refuge!
You're a proven help in time of trouble—
more than enough and always
available whenever I need You.

PSALM 46:1, TPT

I name this day REFUGE. He covers me with His feathers and under the shadow of His wing I take refuge. His truth is my shield. I do not fear the enemy's arrows. I do not fear fiery darts.

I am sheltered, protected, defended. He goes before me and is my rear guard. Through Him I have the victory. He causes me to win. In Him I prevail. He is my REFUGE!

Sit down in God's presence today. Spend the night in Shaddai's shadow. Let Him cover you, shield you, protect and defend you. He is your home.

DEEP WELL

Joyfully you'll pull up buckets of water from the wells of salvation. And as you do it, you'll say, "Give thanks to God. Call out His name. Ask Him anything! Shout to the nations, tell them what He's done, spread the news of His great reputation!"

ISAIAH 12:3-4, MSG

I name this day DEEP WELL. I am a deep well and I have joyously drawn waters from the well of salvation.

I am a well-watered tree. I am connected to rivers of living water, so even when all around me is dry, my bucket of trust has access to cool, clear, refreshing water.

I am washed in the water of the Word. I embrace wisdom and understanding. Therefore, I can draw out and call out the purposes of God in others. I am a DEEP WELL.

In Genesis 26, Isaac reopened and dug again the wells that had been dug by his father, Abraham because they were full of sand, blocking access to the water. Is there a filled-in well in your life? No more shallows, it is time to dig deep!

PEACE

Don't fret or worry. Instead of worrying, pray. Let petitions and praises shape your worries into prayers, letting God know your concerns. Before you know it, a sense of God's wholeness, everything coming together for good, will come and settle you down. It's wonderful what happens when Christ displaces worry at the center of your life.

PHILIPPIANS 4:6-7, MSG

I name this day PEACE. It is like a wide, calm, life-giving river flooding my soul. Blessing and provision float down that river.

The peace of God surpasses my understanding—it shows up even in chaos, in the middle of the most trying circumstances. Peace is not the absence of something, but rather the presence of Someone. It is not a feeling, it is a person—the Prince of Peace.

Peace guards my heart and mind, quieting my soul. I will bring peace with me today because I carry the Prince of Peace in me. Today, I rest in God's amazing PEACE.

Where do you need to experience God's peace? What anxieties or cares do you need to lay at His feet today? Let Him settle you down. Drink in His wholeness.

ULTIMATE

*Now to Him who is able to do exceedingly abundantly
above all that we ask or think, according to the power
that works in us, to Him be glory in the church by Christ
Jesus to all generations, forever and ever. Amen.*

EPHESIANS 3:20-21, NKJV

I name this day ULTIMATE. I expect it to unfold in the best way imaginable. I believe great things will happen today and open myself up for amazing coincidences to occur.

I step into God's promise for exceedingly abundantly above what I ask or think to show up and totally blow me away. I will actively search for golden opportunities and divine appointments. When they appear, I will faithfully seize them.

Something big is in the wind. Something huge is hovering. I don't know what, but I have set the dial on my awareness to ULTIMATE!

ULTIMATE: *the best achievable
or imaginable of its kind.*

Can you feel your expectations rising? Can you connect with God's heart to give you more than you dared ask for? His eyes are on you— look for Him today!

ABOUND IN LOVE

*The Lord is gracious and merciful, slow to
anger and abounding in steadfast love.*

PSALM 145:8, ESV

I name this day ABOUND IN LOVE. I am saved by God's gracious intervention. I feel His face shining on me. I sense His pleasure.

I declare graciousness to flow out of me towards all I encounter today. May my countenance be gentle. May my words be pleasant; as sweet and as nutritious as a honeycomb.

I am courteous. I am kind. I ABOUND IN LOVE.

Have you ever been around someone whose words were pleasant and their countenance was sweet? Focus on God's pleasure in you and yours will be too!

GLAD

You have put more joy in my heart than they
have when their grain and wine abound.

PSALM 4:7, ESV

I name this day GLAD. This is the day that the Lord has made I will rejoice and be glad in it!

I am happy. I choose cheerful. I look for the joy in things and keep myself open for humor, for laughter, and for glee. I will spread love and light wherever I go.

I make a difference. I shift atmospheres. I lighten the load by bringing the countenance and pleasure of God into situations. I am GLAD!

Have you ever watched puppies play? Or baby goats? How about an infant first finding its fingers and toes? That's gladness. Experience that joy and cheer today.

COMPASSION

Put on then, as God's chosen ones, holy and beloved,
compassionate hearts, kindness, humility, meekness,
and patience, bearing with one another, and if one has
a complaint against another, forgiving each other; as
the Lord has forgiven you, so you also must forgive.

COLOSSIANS 3:12-13, ESV

I name this day COMPASSION. I want to see people, places, and circumstances through the eyes of God.

Where I am quick to judge, let mercy arise. When I have too little patience, let honor flood and color my speech.

Let my passion for people be expressed in compassion over them. I put on kindness, grace, and mercy as my garments today. Let me be aware of "back stories" behind every action or reaction. May love provide the benefit of the doubt in each situation.

Judgment is natural. I need something supernatural. May God's love well up until out of me flows a fountain of COMPASSION.

It is easy to spot a bad attitude, bad behavior, or bad choices and pass judgement. It is harder to remember that the one making them has a story you don't know. Remember today that each person you encounter is God's child—the apple of His eye. Look for opportunities to express your compassion.

TRUST

*Trust in the Lord with all your heart and lean not on
your own understanding; in all your ways submit
to Him, and He will make your paths straight.*

PROVERBS 3:5-6, NIV

I name this day TRUST. Trust requires vulnerability. Trust recognizes there are things which are beyond my control. Trust is the fruit of love.

My life is greater than my goals. My destiny is larger than my dreams. My purpose is bigger than my pain.

I trust You, God, maker of heaven and earth. I relax my mind as my spirit is renewed. You hold the world in Your hands—You certainly hold me too. I place my trust in You. I demonstrate this trust through obedience to Your Word and submission to Your ways. In every area where I struggle to keep the control, help me recognize You are there and remind me I can relinquish these at any time. Today, in You will I TRUST.

Saying we trust God is easy. Stepping out of our desire to manipulate or control outcomes is hard. Will you risk identifying areas where you struggle with trust?

REPLENISHED

Observe the day of rest as a holy day. This is what the Lord your God has commanded you. You have six days to do all your work. The seventh day is the day of rest—a holy day dedicated to the Lord your God.

DEUTERONOMY 5:12-14a, GW

I name this day REPLENISHED. I am a resource poured out, so I will be a wise steward and replenish my body, my soul, and my mind.

Rest is a strategy. Reflection is a gift. I will rehearse blessings today and walk with a heightened sense of gratitude. I speak life into my body. I speak joy into my soul. I speak peace into my spirit.

This is a blessed day. I will fill my mouth with good things and be REPLENISHED.

What restores you? What fills up your tank and recharges you? Even if today does not allow for this activity, pause and plan a time when you can fill up and replenish.

COMMITTED

*For I am sure that neither death nor life, nor angels
nor rulers, nor things present nor things to come,
nor powers, nor height nor depth, nor anything
else in all creation, will be able to separate us
from the love of God in Christ Jesus our Lord.*

ROMANS 8:38-39, ESV

I name this day COMMITTED. My "why" is strong enough to push me through my "what" today. My awareness that I am part of a larger story compels me to show up fully persuaded, fully engaged, and fully connected.

Forgetting the things which are behind me, I look forward to the things which are yet to come. I press toward the mark for the prize of the high calling of God in Christ Jesus. I will stay my course. I will run with honor. I will finish well. I am fully COMMITTED.

What is your "why"? Who is your "why"? Do you have an idea what your high calling is? Take time to visit with God and identify these things.

STAND VICTORIOUS

Now my beloved ones, I have saved these most important truths for last: Be supernaturally infused with strength through your life-union with the Lord Jesus. Stand victorious with the force of His explosive power flowing in and through you.

EPHESIANS 6:10-12, MSG

I name this day STAND VICTORIOUS. I am strong in the Lord and in the power of His might. I will put on God's armor to fight against the strategies of the accuser.

I am more than a conqueror. I am an overcomer. The weapons God gave me are well-crafted from the best materials. He built me for endurance. His power flows through me, and I stand on those promises. I fight in faith. Whatever comes my way, I STAND VICTORIOUS.

Strength training builds bones and muscles through resistance, by putting them under stress. Being built up this way not only increases strength, but lowers the risk of injury. Knowing this, can you identify areas of resistance which God is using to strengthen you so you can stand victriously?

ARISE

*Arise, shine, for your light has come, and the
glory of the Lord has risen upon you.*

ISAIAH 60:1, ESV

I name this day ARISE. Darkness has no hold on me because God's light has come. His glory is on me.

I am His temple, the place of His habitation. I am a living stone. This awareness strikes me dumb. God lives in me. He has chosen to make His home in my heart—it is too wonderful to comprehend.

The glory of God's sunlight breaks over me and nations come to that light, kings to the brightness of my rising. I pour out gifts of worship on an altar of praise. I command my spirit, "Arise, child of God. Break forth into joy. Step into the garments suited for your destiny, He is bathing you, His glorious temple, in splendor—ARISE!"

The world is wrapped in darkness, but God has bathed you in the glorious light of His glory! Let this truth sink in. Let your heart arise, sing and rejoice in reverent jubilee!

RETURN

"... Return to Me," declares the Lord
Almighty, "and I will return to you ..."

ZECHARIAH 1:3, NIV

I name this day RETURN. I anticipate the beauty and majesty of Christ's return to the earth. It makes my heart skip a beat just to ponder the very thought of it!

I long for restoration of things lost and of things that should have been but never were. I anticipate a return of the hearts of sons to fathers, the hearts of daughters to mothers.

In this spirit, I return to my first love today and fellowship with God's presence. I return gratitude to Him for all He has done. His joy calls to me and His kindness beckons my heart and whispers: "My beloved, I am here waiting for you, RETURN."

For what does your heart long for restoration? To where do you desire to return? Everything Jesus did was to provide for our return to the Father.

JANUARY 31

UNCOMMON

But now, O Lord, You are our Father;
we are the clay, and You our potter;
and all we are the work of Your hand.

ISAIAH 64:8, NKJV

I name this day UNCOMMON. I am a significant and differentiated presence in the world. I have been made by God's hand. Special. One of a kind. What I have to share is unique and valuable. What I bring to the world has worth.

I refuse to agree with any word or thought that diminishes the glory of God expressed through me. I will actively agree with what God says about me. With intention, I will act with the character He calls me to embrace. I am UNCOMMON.

UNCOMMON: *not ordinary,*
remarkable, exceptional.

What words or thoughts have you agreed with that diminish the glory of God expressed through you or limit His greatness in you? Spend some time today uncovering these, so you can begin to agree actively with what God says about you.

FEBRUARY

*Now I'm sure of this: the sufferings we endure
now are not even worth comparing to the glory
that is coming and will be revealed in us.*

ROMANS 8:18, VOICE

PREPARATION

"Be ready for action, and have your lamps burning.
Be like servants waiting to open the door at their master's
knock when he returns from a wedding. Blessed are
those servants whom the master finds awake when he
comes. I can guarantee this truth: He will change his
clothes, make them sit down at the table, and serve
them. They will be blessed if he comes in the middle of
the night or toward morning and finds them awake."

LUKE 12:35-38, GW

I name this day PREPARATION. I am intentionally preparing for opportunities I desire to see manifest in my life. I am ready for action, taking specific steps in the direction of my dreams, knowing I will reap in due season if I faint not.

I declare open doors before me and speak favorable outcomes, divine encounters, and miracle interventions. In all labor there is profit, so today's labor is commanded to be profitable.

Opportunity meets preparation, so today I diligently prepare.

What are you preparing for? No matter how big or small, God has divinely placed you in a time of preparation so that you may be a conqueror over it!

START SMALL

*This is a large work I've called you into, but don't be
overwhelmed by it. It's best to start small. Give a cool
cup of water to someone who is thirsty, for instance.
The smallest act of giving or receiving makes you a
true apprentice. You won't lose out on a thing.*

MATTHEW 10:41-42, MSG

I name this day START SMALL. I am a true apprentice, dedicated to a lifetime of honing my craft—giving and receiving. Little acts of kindness, intentional moments of joy.

God has big things in store for me. If I knew what He was calling me to, I probably couldn't bear the burden of responsibility. That's why He leads me step-by-step, building me up so I'll be ready to step into that authority when I am proven.

Great work is possible when I commit to the long haul. It might not look like much today, but I won't despise this meager beginning. I will commit every action to the Lord as I faithfully START SMALL.

Often, it is easy to see the picture printed on the outside of the puzzle box and miss the pieces that the picture is comprised of. However small, don't wait to start putting your pieces together. Trust that from small beginnings come great things.

MOMENTUM

I will press on—moving steadfastly forward along
Your path. I will not look back. I will not stumble.

PSALM 17:5, VOICE

I name this day MOMENTUM. I move forward, one foot in front of the other, knowing that conquering even the small things and gaining mastery over the mundane builds momentum.

I confess excellence as I perform tasks, however great or small. I decree favor and remember faithfulness in the little avails much. I embrace this day's assignment and weigh its value in light of the larger picture of living well and walking worthy. I lean into forward motion today. I move foward in the direction of my destiny, in the pursuit of my dreams, building MOMENTUM.

MOMENTUM: a force that multiplies the
effect of effort.

In which areas of your life do you feel as though you are at a standstill?
The best way to move forward is to take a step in the right direction—
no matter the size, the Lord has called you to keep moving forward!

STEADY

*Those who are proud cruelly ridicule me, but I will
keep to the steady path of Your teachings.*

PSALM 119:51, VOICE

I name this day STEADY. Slow and steady really does win the race. Even if those around me neither notice nor appreciate the changes I am making to improve my future, I will stay the course.

It hurts when those I love don't understand my dreams, and it is harder to reach for them without the power of agreement or the covenant protection of accountability. But I will remain true.

I agree with God and I align my dreams with His. He will protect and keep me with His covenant blessings. He notices my choices to change and celebrates them. In fact, He is singing over me!

I will keep reaching for dreams even if I must do it privately. I will win. My success will confound those very friends and family who cannot find their way to support me now.

I stay the course, solid and STEADY.

Chasing dreams, however big or small, can often feel lonely. In these times, the Comforter walks alongside you, guiding your steps—you need only stay the course. What dreams have you delayed chasing lately? Steady on, stay the course!

WILLING TO LEARN

*Listen well to wise counsel and be willing to learn
from correction so that by the end of your life you'll
be known for your wisdom. A person may have many
ideas concerning God's plan for his life, but only the
designs of God's purpose will succeed in the end.*

PSALM 119:5-6, MSG

I name this day WILLING TO LEARN. Investment in knowing the counsel of God is wise. Heeding that counsel is wiser still. May my walk be solid—rooted and grounded in God's Word. When I compare my life to others, I feel like a miserable failure. When I examine my life with the counsel of God, I have no regrets for keeping on His course.

I will listen well to wise counsel, I will plant my feet firmly on the solid Rock. God, I do not despise correction, I am WILLING TO LEARN.

Have you intentionally rooted yourself within God's Word? What is God's counsel concerning you? Do you have sources of wise counsel? Can you receive correction and adjustment? Make sure that you are able to receive from others and that you are willing to learn.

EVERY CHANCE

Jesus looked hard at them and said, "No chance at all if you think you can pull it off yourself. Every chance in the world if you trust God to do it."

MATTHEW 19:26, MSG

I name this day EVERY CHANCE. I am often tempted to do things in my own strength, for my advancement or protection. Rather than independence or maturity, this actually reveals a lack of trust in God. In my heart, I want to believe He'll come through for me, but more often than I care to admit, I am my own back up plan. I have seen Him show up for others, but I am sometimes afraid He will let me down. So, I try to pull things off on my own.

That is a bad plan. I know on my own I will trip and fall, so today I place my trust in God. By walking closely beside Him and staying under the shadow of His wing, I go from having no chance to having EVERY CHANCE.

The trick to drawing closer to God is not to try harder. Instead of trying harder, try following closer! How might your heart shift if you chose to walk closer to God today?

GOD IS MY SOURCE

*"Be especially careful when you are trying to
be good so that you don't make a performance
out of it. It might be good theater, but the God
who made you won't be applauding."*

MATTHEW 6:1, MSG

I name this day GOD IS MY SOURCE. Everything good I have ever done is because God was at work through me. Only when my nature and character is surrendered to His am I capable of good.

It's funny how I attribute my wins to the exercise of discipline, my intellect, or wise choices, but I blame my flops on people or circumstances beyond my control. In fact, my best days are the ones where I get out of the way and submit to God's good pleasure, allowing Him to work through me. With humble grace, I gratefully acknowledge that GOD IS MY SOURCE.

Without God, nothing is possible—but WITH God, everything is possible! You access this power by surrendering your life to His ways. In what areas do you need to surrender? Where do you need to acknowledge Him as your source?

SUFFICIENT GRACE

But He said to me, "My grace is sufficient for you, for My power is made perfect in weakness." Therefore I will boast all the more gladly of my weaknesses, so that the power of Christ may rest upon me.

2 CORINTHIANS 12:9, ESV

I name this day SUFFICIENT GRACE. I will drink it in. I will spill it out onto others. I will rejoice in God's abundant supply. Rather than hiding from my weakness, I recognize the supernatural gift of God's perfecting power when I surrender my weakness to Him without shame, blame, or excuse.

Your grace is sufficient for me. God, I desire that Your power may rest upon me. Therefore, I humbly, willingly, and gratefully receive Your amazing, SUFFICIENT GRACE.

You are saved through God's sufficient grace, and you always have access to it, even when you feel undeserving of it. How can you share this amazing, sufficient grace of God with someone today?

HOPE IN THE LORD

But those who hope in the Lord will renew their strength.
They will soar on wings like eagles; they will run and
not grow weary, they will walk and not be faint.

ISAIAH 40:31, NIV

I name this day HOPE IN THE LORD. May God renew my strength and may His grace lift me up until I soar like an eagle. May I run my race without weariness, and walk life's path without growing faint.

Hope anchors my soul and is the seedbed for faith. Hope stirs my expectations that He will cause all things to work together for my good. Hope placed in other things will fail, so I put my HOPE IN THE LORD.

Has misplaced hope left you weary? Take time today to pause and soak in the never-ending, life-changing hope of God. Let it refresh and renew your spirit.

CULTIVATE CHARACTER

Cultivate these things. Immerse yourself in them.
The people will all see you mature right before their
eyes! Keep a firm grasp on both your character and your
teaching. Don't be diverted. Just keep at it. Both you
and those who hear you will experience salvation.

1 TIMOTHY 4:15-16, MSG

I name this day CULTIVATE CHARACTER. I will immerse myself in things which develop me, mature me, and cause me to grow. I will faithfully steward my heart.

Though I do not enjoy afflictions, I recognize each as a gift—an opportunity for my character to be strengthened and refined. My heart is wild and free, but my character is best when submitted to the loving nurture and pruning of the Holy Spirit. I make it my prayer that I yield my untamed parts to the Master Gardner and willingly allow Him to CULTIVATE CHARACTER.

The best way to cultivate character is to step outside of your comfort zone. Instead of leaning into comfort, lean into cultivation. Growth is challenging. Change is hard, but the payoff is a reward worth working for.

PRUNE BACK

*Every branch in me that does not produce fruit He
removes, and He prunes every branch that produces
fruit so that it will produce even more fruit.*

JOHN 15:2, CSB

I name this day PRUNE BACK. Only those things which bear no fruit do I completely cut off. That which is fruit bearing, I assess. By evaluating and carefully trimming, I set it up to be even more fruitful.

There are times when I feel "cut back," and it is uncomfortable. After a period of dynamic growth and fruitfulness, submitting to being pruned requires swallowing my pride and allowing a season of dormant rest. In that time, I am still. My roots stretch down deep and send nourishment up and through every branch of my life.

With gentleness, with insight, and great care for the wholeness and health of all my parts, tenderly, I PRUNE BACK.

When was the last time you pruned yourself back? Are you holding onto branches that bear no fruit? Assess your "fruit" today. If it does not bear fruit, prune it back!

WORK WELL

Work willingly at whatever you do, as though you were working for the Lord rather than for people.

COLOSSIANS 3:23, NLT

I name this day WORK WELL. May I demonstrate diligence in the details, treat both people and projects with focused attention, and finish my day knowing I gave it my best.

I desire fortunate outcomes and wish to be found a profitable servant. I want to go beyond satisfactory and enter the realm of excellence. Whatever work I do today, may I WORK WELL.

God is honored by your best work. Instead of doing a hundred things at fifty percent, try doing a few important things at one hundred percent. Commit your work to the Lord. Walk in a spirit of excellence and watch what God does!

PROVISION WHILE I REST

*The ravens brought him bread and meat
in the morning and bread and meat in the
evening, and he drank from the brook.*

1 KINGS 17:6, NIV

I name this day PROVISION WHILE I REST. Sometimes the tyranny of the urgent causes me to push, push, push. It seems that my answer to every question about how I am is, "Busy!" That isn't God's highest and best for me. He wants me to make rest part of my regular rhythm.

My unwillingness to surrender to down time is based in fear—fear that there won't be enough income if I don't keep a breakneck pace. But just as God brought ravens bearing food to Elijah, He will sustain me in my season beside the brook.

The One who knows my end from my beginning cares enough to ensure PROVISION WHILE I REST.

Even while you rest, the Provider champions on your behalf. Open your hands to the many splendors that the Provider wants to bless you with today. Trust Him and rest.

PATHS OF RIGHTEOUSNESS

The Lord is my shepherd; I shall not want.
He makes me lie down in green pastures.
He leads me beside still waters. He restores my soul.
He leads me in paths of righteousness for His name's sake.

PSALM 23:1-3, ESV

I name this day PATHS OF RIGHTEOUSNESS. May I follow God's course, trusting that He leads me every step of the way.

The more I follow Him, the more often I am willing to lie down in green pastures and be restored. When I am restored, I am stronger, braver, kinder, and have greater clarity. Little things don't get under my skin, and I have the ability to remain calm and focused—even when under pressure.

He's the Good Shepherd. He knows the lay of the land and has a plan for where He wants to lead me. I'm in no hurry. I will enjoy the still waters and wait for Him to guide me along PATHS OF RIGHTEOUSNESS.

Is your soul at rest? Do you feel anxious before the day has even begun, or are you able to greet the Good Shepherd with joy in the morning? Rest is a strategy. Trusting God to lead you allows you the courage to rest. He'll provide, protect, and prepare for you.

RECEIVE WHAT YOU GIVE

We all live off His generous abundance, gift after gift
after gift. We got the basics from Moses, and then His
exuberant giving and receiving, This endless knowing and
understanding—all this came through Jesus, the Messiah.

JOHN 1:16-17, MSG

I name this day RECEIVE WHAT YOU GIVE—gratefully, joyfully, trusting Your provision and plan. I will not question my blessings or insult You, the Giver, by wishing for different gifts than You have given.

God, I'm sorry for all the times I have wanted what You gave someone else. I repent of every time I have complained or cursed my blessings. Like a selfish child afraid to share my toys, I have grabbed at Your gifts like they are the last ones I'll ever receive. I know Your heart towards me is full of extravagant generosity.

With a glad and thankful heart, I RECEIVE WHAT YOU GIVE.

Are you holding onto receipts for the gifts God has given you, maybe hoping to exchange them for something better? Regardless of what you have been given, choose to receive with open hands instead of closed fists. Be grateful and filled with joy.

MADE CLEAN

*I will sprinkle clean water on you, and you shall be clean
from all your uncleannesses, and from all your idols I
will cleanse you. And I will give you a new heart, and
a new spirit I will put within you. And I will remove the
heart of stone from your flesh and give you a heart of
flesh. And I will put My Spirit within you, and cause you
to walk in My statutes and be careful to obey My rules.*

EZEKIEL 36:25-27, ESV

I name this day MADE CLEAN. What I do when no one is looking is who I really am. Let me put on no airs or pretend piety.

I want to clear out the closets of my heart, get the dirt in the corners, and clean all the places no one else sees. Sprinkle me, and I will be cleansed. Give me a new heart and put a new spirit within me.

May I resist the temptation to *appear* righteous, but instead live rightly for You alone. Give me a heart of flesh, put Your Spirit in me. Wash me and I will be MADE CLEAN.

It is easy to be good when people are paying attention. How clean is your heart in secret, where no one sees? Pray that He will create a clean heart in you today, restore a right spirit, and draw you close to His side.

DETERMINE MY STEPS

We can make our plans,
but the LORD determines our steps.

PROVERBS 16:9, NLT

I name this day DETERMINE MY STEPS. Faithfully I make plans—good ones—considering my place in humanity and desiring to make a difference for good. Humbly I submit all my plans to You, Father.

When I commit my work to the Lord, and my plans are established. I count the costs and proceed in wisdom. I seek Your counsel as well as the advice of godly counselors. I make all my plans with Your heart in mind, gratefully acknowledging it is You who will DETERMINE MY STEPS.

Though we may make our plans, God orders our steps. What areas of your life do you need to offer up to the Father so that your steps can be determined?

DO GOOD

See that no one pays back with evil for evil, but always
seek to do good to one another and to everyone.

1 THESSALONIANS 5:15, ESV

I name this day DO GOOD. In all the places and spaces where I find myself, with all the people with whom I am privileged to cross paths, my aim is to be a blessing.

I was created in Christ Jesus for good works. God prepared these good works for me, and when I let my light shine by doing them, others see them and give glory to my Father.

I work heartily. I am mindful of my motivations and I have purposed in my heart today that I will DO GOOD.

When was the last time you did a random act of kindness? Today, I challenge you to one act of kindness. Walk in the call to do good to others today!

ABUNDANTLY BLESSED

*The one who blesses others is abundantly
blessed; those who help others are helped.*

PROVERBS 11:25, MSG

*The generous soul will be made rich, and he
who waters will also be watered himself.*

PROVERBS 11:25, NKJV

I name this day ABUNDANTLY BLESSED. I am blessed so that I might
be a blessing. My soul is generous. I water others every chance I
get and whenever I am parched, God sends someone with water
to refresh me.

My eyes are searching, looking for who and when and how I can
extend blessings and help. With gratitude and joy, I acknowledge I
am ABUNDANTLY BLESSED.

*When you pour the blessings you've been given onto others, your
cup will soon overflow! What blessing will you choose to share with
someone today?*

LOOK UP

So if you're serious about living this new resurrection life with Christ, act like it. Pursue the things over which Christ presides. Don't shuffle along, eyes to the ground, absorbed with the things right in front of you. Look up, and be alert to what is going on around Christ—that's where the action is. See things from His perspective.

COLOSSIANS 3:1-2, MSG

I name this day LOOK UP—up from the daily grind, up from the cares and worries, up from the endless tasks. It is too easy to become absorbed in the day's news, the routine at the office, and the mundane responsibilities of taking care of business. There is more.

Today I shall be on the alert. I look through the eyes of the Spirit searching for Christ at work. That's the work in which I want to participate. First, I must shift my perspective and LOOK UP.

Are you looking inward or upward? Though this world is full of distractions, look up and be a witness to His perfect love. Look up and gain His point of view!

KEEP NOTHING BACK

Open up before God, keep nothing back; He'll do whatever needs to be done: He'll validate your life in the clear light of day and stamp you with approval at high noon.

PSALM 37:5-6, MSG

I name this day KEEP NOTHING BACK. I open myself up to God, risking becoming fully known in order to be fully loved. I never need to fear that what He sees in me will change His love for me. His love is unchanging. His acceptance of me is based on His covenant with me and not my performance. What a relief!

Masks are pointless with God. All they do is limit my view of His face, they hide nothing from Him. He is patient and always has eternity in mind. He will perfect that which concerns me. If I will allow, God will do the work in me that needs to be done. Today as I come before the throne, I will KEEP NOTHING BACK.

When was the last time that you felt fully seen? As you go about your day, seek out opportunities to be fully known, fully present, fully YOU. Watch how God honors your authenticity and works in your heart.

RESET

*For if a man is in Christ he becomes a new person altogether—the
past is finished and gone, everything has become fresh and new.*

2 CORINTHIANS 5:17, PHILLIPS

I name this day RESET. I am not my best self every day. Some days
my unredeemed nature grabs the mic, and my broadcast to the
world in the moment does not reflect the character of Christ or the
identity He gave me. Authenticity does not mean I give permission
to allow the raw, unfiltered me to have center stage. It means I see
that raw work for what it is, bring it back under subjection to God's
Spirit, and command it to congruently align with my redeemed
nature. It requires that I remain transparent through the process.
I am a work in progress. Growing through change, being daily
transformed, renewing my mind, and consecrating my actions. On
days when I blow it, I have the throne of grace fully accessible to
me and the fresh mercies of God fully available.

Old things (thought patterns, speech, habits) are passed away and
the new (thought patterns, speech, habits) have come. I declare
this day is a RESET to my redeemed nature.

---

*His forgiveness is unconditional—when you stumble, He will pick you
back up, dust you off, and walk beside you. Put on the mind of Christ.
Put on the armor of God. Stand fast on your most holy faith. Walk
worthy of your calling. Amen.*

CLEAN BREAK

With promises like this to pull us on, dear friends, let's make a clean break with everything that defiles or distracts us, both within and without. Let's make our entire lives fit and holy temples for the worship of God.

2 CORINTHIANS 7:1, MSG

I name this day CLEAN BREAK. If my kitchen is full of junk food, no matter how hard I try to eat well, I'll give in to that stuff lying around. It's the same with my spirit. If I let unforgiveness, offense, irritation, pride, or idolatry in proximity, I soon embrace my old nature and become hopelessly distracted.

I am meant to be a temple for the living God. So, with everything that defiles or distracts me from within or without, today I make a CLEAN BREAK.

What is keeping you from holiness? Today, I pray that the Lord will make this clearer to you so you can surrender it, allow God to cut it away—a clean break—and restore your focus on Him.

CALLED BLESSED

Her children rise up and call her blessed;
her husband also, and he praises her.

PROVERBS 31:28, NIV

I name this day CALLED BLESSED. Not that I deserve it because I am flawed and imperfect and fall down often. But because of grace, for the mystery of love, and the commitment of lasting, meaningful connection.

All the good things in my life come from God. It is with humble gratitude that I have been CALLED BLESSED.

Through every triumph and stumble, you are loved by a God who fully knows your heart. His love is all-encompassing; it draws no lines and bears no shame. You are called blessed, always and forever. Take time today to breathe this in.

WELL REPRESENTED

*Let the peace of Christ keep you in tune with each other,
in step with each other. None of this going off and doing
your own thing. And cultivate thankfulness. Let the Word
of Christ—the Message—have the run of the house. Give
it plenty of room in your lives. Instruct and direct one
another using good common sense. And sing, sing your
hearts out to God! Let every detail in your lives—words,
actions, whatever—be done in the name of the Master,
Jesus, thanking God the Father every step of the way.*

COLOSSIANS 3:15-17, MSG

I name this day WELL REPRESENTED. May all I do or say reflect that Christ lives in me and is at work in my life. His peace leaks out of me and brings peace to those who get close to me. My heart is full of thanksgiving, and I carry the atmosphere of heaven with me at all times.

As God's ambassador, wherever I go and with whomever I interact, may heaven's kingdom be WELL REPRESENTED.

In what area of your life do you feel like you represent Christ well? Similarly, in what areas do you feel you could represent Him better? You are an heir to His throne—straighten your crown and walk with your God-given authority. Represent Him well.

SIMPLE HUMILITY

God's righteousness doesn't grow from human anger.
So throw all spoiled virtue and cancerous evil
in the garbage. In simple humility, let our
gardener, God, landscape you with the Word,
making a salvation-garden of your life.

JAMES 1:20-21, MSG

I name this day SIMPLE HUMILITY. I yield to the Gardener. I make this my prayer: plow me, make straight furrows, plant seeds, cover me, weed, water, and fertilize my life until my salvation-garden is lush with fruitful produce!

God, I yield my prideful efforts and receive Your gifts with SIMPLE HUMILITY.

HUMILITY: *freedom from pride or arrogance, a*
modest view of one's own importance.

Though it is easy to boast in the fruit you reap, it's important to point the accolades to the Gardener! It is not your efforts, but His alone. How can you exchange your pride for SIMPLE HUMILITY?

SURRENDERED

*Do you not know that your bodies are temples of
the Holy Spirit, who is in you, who you have received
from God? You are not your own; you were bought
at a price. Therefore, honor God with your bodies.*

1 CORINTHIANS 6:19-20, NIV

I name this day SURRENDERED. When I am fully surrendered, I am most powerful, I am most free.

I decree my will to bow to God's great purpose, His unfailing grace, and His timing. I submit my plans to His design and acknowledge His master plan. Break me. Melt me. Mold me. Fill me. I am Thine, totally and completely SURRENDERED.

What is keeping you from surrendering everything to God? What are you holding back, afraid to give Him? Throughout the day, dream with God about how being fully surrendered could revolutionize your life!

DIFFERENT KIND OF SACRIFICE

Make sure you don't take things for granted and go slack in working for the common good; share what you have with others. God takes particular pleasure in acts of worship—a different kind of "sacrifice"—that take place in kitchen and workplace and on the streets.

HEBREWS 13:16, MSG

I name this day DIFFERENT KIND OF SACRIFICE. May my work be worship. May my loving others be loving God. May I take nothing for granted, be grateful for even the small things, complain about nothing.

Let me demonstrate the love of God through acts of service, words of kindness, making sure others are seen, heard, and valued. Today I will be intentional about offering a DIFFERENT KIND OF SACRIFICE.

When you draw closer to God, your heart will align with His heart. Let everything you do from now on be glorifying to Him, reflecting the Good News He has given you! Let your sacrifice of worship be demonstrated in the kitchen and on the streets.

CLEANSED AND GRATEFUL LIFE

Jesus reached out and touched him,
saying, "I want to be clean."
Then and there, all signs of the leprosy were gone.
Jesus said, "Don't talk about this all over town.
Just quietly present your healed body to the priest,
along with the appropriate expressions of thanks
to God. Your cleansed and grateful life, not your
words, will bear witness to what I have done."

MATTHEW 8:3-4, MSG

I name this day CLEANSED AND GRATEFUL LIFE. With expressions of thanks to God, may I bear witness of Him without words. May my life be a living epistle, testifying of God's goodness and faithfulness. May my love bear witness of His love.

May I fill the earth with appropriate expressions of thanks to God and reflect His light through a CLEANSED AND GRATEFUL LIFE.

When was the last time you came to God with thanks instead of a list? Today, recall the many ways God has demonstrated His great love for you. List them—count your blessings. Then let your life demonstrate that you are cleansed and grateful.

MARCH

Let the word of the Anointed One richly inhabit your lives. With all wisdom teach, counsel, and instruct one another. Sing the psalms, compose hymns and songs inspired by the Spirit, and keep on singing—sing to God from hearts full and spilling over with thankfulness.

COLOSSIANS 3:16, VOICE

INCREASE

*I will certainly bless you. I will multiply your
descendants beyond number, like the stars in
the sky and the sand on the seashore.*

GENESIS 22:17, NLT

I name this day INCREASE. I am blessed coming in and blessed going out. I am blessed in both city and field. Whatever I put my hand to prospers.

I decree increase over my finances. I declare increase over my opportunities. I speak an increase of my awareness, my understanding, and my ability to apply wisdom. This day I will see INCREASE.

In what areas of life do you long for increase? God gives good gifts to His children, and that certainly includes you! He will bless you abundantly— no conditions attached! Today, choose a mindset of value, wealth, and increase!

GENEROSITY IS JOY

The eyes of the Lord search the whole
earth in order to strengthen those whose
hearts are fully committed to Him ...

2 CHRONICLES 16:9, NLT

I name this day GENEROSITY IS JOY. God, You take care of Your own—Your eyes are always searching to and fro. I will be Your hands and feet, the expression of Your blessing on earth.

I am a conduit and not a container. The glory of God flows through my life to touch a lost and hurting world. Pour through me, God, GENEROSITY IS JOY!

You are called to give with a joyful heart! There is no need to protect what you have; you can seek out ways to give generously. As God has given to you, be a living example of a joyfully generous creation!

COMMIT MY WORK

*Commit your work to the Lord,
and your plans will be established.*

PROVERBS 16:3, ESV

I name this day COMMIT MY WORK. May all I put my hands to be in service to something and someone greater. I pledge my faithfulness in my employment. That which I do, I do as an ambassador, representing the kingdom of heaven.

Let my plans be established by God as to Him I COMMIT MY WORK.

What tasks are you putting your hands to today? This day, you are given the choice to honor God in all that you do. Whatever it is, it can be done to His glory, for service in His kingdom. Take a moment to commit the work of your hands to God today.

WELCOME HERE

*Therefore welcome one another as Christ has
welcomed you, for the glory of God.*

ROMANS 15:7, ESV

I name this day WELCOME HERE. How comforting to know God is available to me—in fact, He stands knocking at my door and calling my name! Willingly I swing wide the door and invite Him in.

It is my honor and my privilege that You, God, would make Your home in me. I hold nothing back from Your presence, and I invite others to come inside, to taste and see that You are good. Access is granted to every room, for You are WELCOME HERE!

Because of the provisions made by the Father for you, you are welcome in His courts, and He makes His home in you. That invitation can embolden you to not only welcome Him in your heart, but to invite others into His presence with you. Bid Him enter today.

AT THE TABLE

Jesus saith unto them, "Come and dine ..."
JOHN 21:12a, KJV

I name this day AT THE TABLE—a sacred altar where community is formed, where bread is broken, where truth is spoken, and where hearts connect. Jesus calls, I answer.

He has spread a table before me. He has cared for all my needs. I have been comforted by His hospitality and felt the joy of belonging. I have an assignment; as He has made room for me, I am called to make room for others AT THE TABLE.

The Father has made ample room at His table for you, and in turn has called you to make a place at the table for others. Who are you making room for at your table?

CAPACITY

"Enlarge the place of your tent, stretch your curtains wide, do not hold back; lengthen your cords, strengthen your stakes. For you will spread out to the right and to the left; your descendants will dispossess nations and settle in their desolate cities."

ISAIAH 54:2-3, NIV

I name this day CAPACITY. I stretch out my tent pegs and enlarge the place of my territory. I recognize my capacity for growth is larger than I can possibly imagine. I expand my expectation and command expansion and increase in my life for God's glory.

I refuse to allow my mind to be the limitation of God's power at work in me. I decree love to stretch me, as a growing baby stretches the womb. Holy Spirit fill me fresh. Today I place a demand on my potential. I refuse to settle, and I reach for the possibilities that come when I explore my CAPACITY.

Expanding your capacity will be uncomfortable at first, but God has called you to deeper and higher places. In what areas have you settled for comfort over your calling? S-t-r-e-t-c-h. Make room for more of Him in you!

POSITION YOURSELF

"You do not have to fight in this battle. Position yourselves, stand still and see the salvation of the Lord, who is with you, Judah and Jerusalem. Do not be afraid or discouraged. Tomorrow, go out to face them, for the LORD is with you."

2 CHRONICLES 20:17, CSB

I name this day POSITION YOURSELF. Become poised between heaven and earth with your face turned towards God and the magnitude of His glory. Without fear or dismay, stand still in His presence; loved, cared for, protected, provided for.

You don't need to strive to earn God's favor or attention. You don't have to fight every battle. God says you need not fear. He says not to be discouraged. In the middle of all you are facing, your assignment from Him is simply to POSITION YOURSELF.

Be still and turn your thoughts toward the Lord. As you acknowledge the sacrifice Jesus made and stand in grateful surrender, you cannot help but break into worship, and in that place of surrender, you are positioned to receive from the Father.

CLEAR DISTINCTIONS

Jesus then said, "I came into the world to bring
everything into the clear light of day, making all
the distinctions clear, so that those who have never
seen will see, and those who have made a great
pretense of seeing will be exposed as blind."

JOHN 9:39, MSG

I name this day CLEAR DISTINCTIONS. Open my eyes, Father, and let me see. Search my heart and reveal to me hidden things and warped ideas. I want to worship You as You are, not as I imagine You to be. So, show me Your glory. Reveal Yourself to me through loving self-disclosure by the Holy Spirit.

Untwist my midnight thoughts in the light of Your presence and bring me to a place of making CLEAR DISTINCTIONS.

Through Christ, all things are brought to light! What ideas, thoughts, or feelings need to be brought to the light today? When we have wrong ideas about God, it warps how we receive from Him. What thoughts need to be made clear to you?

FRESH STRENGTH

*Why would you ever complain, O Jacob, or, whine, Israel, saying,
"God has lost track of me. He doesn't care what happens to
me"? Don't you know anything? Haven't you been listening?
God doesn't come and go. God lasts. He's Creator of all you
can see or imagine. He doesn't get tired out, doesn't pause to
catch his breath. And He knows everything, inside and out. He
energizes those who get tired, gives fresh strength to dropouts.
For even young people tire and drop out, young folk in their
prime stumble and fall. But those who wait upon God get
fresh strength. They spread their wings and soar like eagles,
they run and don't get tired, they walk and don't lag behind.*

ISAIAH 40:27-31, MSG

I name this day FRESH STRENGTH. What a miracle it is that God
never tires, never pauses to catch His breath. This is beyond my
comprehension. God, you know exactly what I need—even before
I know it. I'm tired. Please show up for me today in power and in
might. Let your joy course through my veins until my strength is
renewed.

I trust you know all and I wait on you to energize me, replenish me
in my weariness, and bring to me the promise you gave for FRESH
STRENGTH.

---

*Do you find yourself trying to keep up with the pace of the world? Wait
on God. Trust His process. Trust His plan. He will show up for you today
and fill you with fresh strength.*

OVER ALL THINGS

We adore You as the One who is over all things.

1 CHRONICLES 29:11, NLT

I name this day OVER ALL THINGS. God, You are my banner. Your banner over me is love. For by You and in You and through You are all things. You've got it covered, I don't know why I continue to worry and be anxious. Help me to trust You more.

What a relief to know my Father, God, is OVER ALL THINGS.

God has dominion over all things, and He is constantly orchestrating them for YOUR good! Live in this promise today: God has overcome the world so that you could be a conqueror within it!

ROOTS NEAR RIVERS

*But blessed is the man who trusts Me, GOD, the woman
who sticks with GOD. They're like trees replanted in Eden,
putting down roots near the rivers—never a worry through
the hottest of summers, never dropping a leaf, serene and
calm through droughts, bearing fresh fruit every season.*

JEREMIAH 17:7-8, MSG

I name this day ROOTS NEAR RIVERS. God, replant me in Eden, restore me to the Garden. Oh, that I might be serene and calm through droughts and able to bear fresh fruit in all seasons. Wouldn't it be wonderful not to worry when life heats up? Wouldn't it be awesome if I was as calm in a dry season as I am when things are going well on every side? Only You can do that in me. Only You.

Only by trusting in You will I be as confident, calm, and serene as a tree with ROOTS NEAR RIVERS.

When you plant your roots near the river of God, you will never rot or run dry. God is in the restoration business! Will you stick with God today? Will you allow yourself to be planted near the river of life? Fresh fruit in every season—amen.

LIFE-GIVING WELL

The mouth of a good person is a deep, life-giving well,
but the mouth of the wicked is a dark cave of abuse.

PROVERBS 10:11, MSG

I name this day LIFE-GIVING WELL. I dug and dug, way down deep. All along the way I was emptying all the dirt (flesh) until I found and tapped into the rivers of living water which never run dry.

I have a river of life flowing out of me! May all who draw from me find a cup of cold, refreshing water offered freely from my LIFE-GIVING WELL.

If you feel dry today, dig your well a little deeper. A river of living water runs through you, and it never runs dry! You are a deep well. Your life brings refreshment to others and this pleases your Father in heaven.

MARCH 13

GRACIOUS SPEECH

*Gracious speech is like clover honey—good taste
to the soul, quick energy for the body.*

PROVERBS 16:24, MSG

I name this day GRACIOUS SPEECH. My words matter. I set the atmosphere by them—their tone and their intent. I recognize their power, so I won't be careless with them. They are like little soldiers I send out into the earth to accomplish the desires of my heart.

Therefore, I will watch my words with all diligence. I want my words to be sweet like honey, good for the soul, positive energy to the body. Today, I set myself to respond to everyone I encounter with GRACIOUS SPEECH.

Do your words act like honey to the soul for others? Don't forget the power of your words today—out of your mouth comes blessings or curses. Choose to spill blessings out like sweet honey. Let the words of your mouth be acceptable in His sight today.

AS I HAVE LOVED YOU

*"Let me give you a new command: Love one another.
In the same way I loved you, you love one another.
This is how everyone will recognize that you are My
disciples—when they see the love you have for each other."*

JOHN 13:34-35, MSG

I name this day AS I HAVE LOVED YOU. When I remember, God, how You have loved me, then loving others is easier. In the light of Your great love, my dark heart becomes bright enough to find the capacity to love.

Jesus, I hear and obey Your command to love the Father and to love others AS I HAVE LOVED YOU.

Loving God, loving others, even loving yourself as He has loved you can feel daunting. Let me encourage you—you are up to the task. Meditate on the extravagant love God has for you. Let it pour over you until you cannot help but spill it out on others.

DEEP-SPIRITED FRIEND

If you've gotten anything at all out of following Christ, if His love has made any difference in your life, if being in a community of the Spirit means anything to you, if you have a heart, if you care—then do me a favor: Agree with each other, love each other, be deep-spirited friends. Don't push your way to the front; don't sweet-talk your way to the top. Put yourself aside, and help others get ahead. Don't be obsessed with getting your own advantage. Forget yourselves long enough to lend a helping hand.

PHILIPPIANS 2:1-4, MSG

I name this day DEEP-SPIRITED FRIEND—the kind I long for, the kind I wish to be. May I forget myself and bring others up; stand in agreement, encourage, help, support, and defend.

In a world infected with narcissism and addicted to superficial interaction, fostering meaningful connections with others is a challenge. But, my friendships are priceless. These people are valuable to me, and I want to show them how grateful I am God has put them in my life. If there is nothing else that can be said about me, may I be known as a DEEP-SPIRITED FRIEND.

Do you find it challenging to forget yourself in order to lift others up? Selflessly helping others is one of your highest calls. Take a moment to thank God for your true friendships. Reach out to one of them today and connect. How will you practice being a deep-spirited friend to them?

DIVINE ACTS

"You've been with me all this time, Philip, and you still don't understand? To see Me is to see the Father. So how can you ask, 'Where is the Father?' Don't you believe that I am in the Father and the Father is in Me? The words that I speak to you aren't mere words. I don't just make them up on My own. The Father who resides in Me crafts each word into a divine act."

JOHN 14:9-10, MSG

I name this day DIVINE ACTS. May the words I speak echo the time spent with you, Father, and the communication between my heart and Yours. Let my thoughts be so saturated in Your love that my words are not my own—may You be the originator.

May I be able to say that the Father who resides in me crafts my words into DIVINE ACTS.

Are your thoughts, words, and actions reflective of your communion with God? How can you better align your communication with God's heart? Imagine God crafting your words into divine acts!

CHOICES

Your word is a lamp for my steps;
it lights the path before me.

PSALM 119:105, VOICE

I name this day CHOICES. Every choice I make takes me toward something and away from something else, so I will make them with careful intention. I will not abdicate my responsibility or yield the privilege of choosing. I will not procrastinate and therefore limit the quality of my options.

I decree wisdom over all my decisions today. I command my awareness to rise and my ability to see far into the distance be strengthened. I declare prudence to be my friend and take God's Word as a lamp for my feet and a light for my path. Today, I make intentional, wise CHOICES.

Where are your choices taking you today? Your choices matter. Will you agree with God? Will you let Him guide your footsteps? Remember, not choosing is a choice. The choices you make today will create the life you live tomorrow. Choose well.

MAKE THE MOST OF IT

Don't miss a trick. Make the most of every opportunity.
Be gracious in your speech. The goal is to
bring out the best in others in a conversation,
not put them down, not cut them out.

COLOSSIANS 4:5-6, MSG

I name this day MAKE THE MOST OF IT. I will leverage every opportunity to be and to share love. I will bring out the best in others, building them up. I will be gracious in my speech, kind in my actions, thoughtful and measured as I go about my day.

Whatever comes my way, I will MAKE THE MOST OF IT!

How might your day unfold if you allowed God's love to cause you to highlight His highest and best in others? What would it look like today if you made the most of every opportunity?

CONTENT AND CAREFREE

So be content with who you are, and don't put on airs.
God's strong hand is on you; He'll promote you at the right
time. Live carefree before God; He is most careful with you.

1 PETER 5:6-7, MSG

I name this day CONTENT AND CAREFREE. I trust the strong hand of God and commit myself to His care. I lay down any ideas to push my way to the top or to try to gain favorable attention from others. When I am tempted to manipulate circumstance to gain an advantage, I'll remember that Your hand is on me and You'll promote me when the time is right.

Anything I have to manipulate to get, I'll have to manipulate to keep. So, by God's grace I embrace the miraculous freedom to live CONTENT AND CAREFREE.

When you cast your cares on the Lord, your weight is lifted! You can enjoy the splendor of His riches and glory. What area are you tempted to manipulate people or circumstances for advancement or promotion? Yield this to His strong hand.

HUMOR

He will fill your mouth with laughter
and your lips with happy shouting.

JOB 8:21, GW

I name this day HUMOR. I choose not to take myself or my circumstances too seriously. God, help me find the funny in the everyday things. Let me laugh—a deep, belly laugh that scrubs my emotions and leaves me smiling even after it subsides.

Today I will allow my soul the opportunity of joy. I declare laughter to arise in my spirit. I release the joy of the Lord into my mind and into the atmosphere everywhere I go. I will look for humor in everyday situations, and I will let myself be childlike enough to enjoy the joke. Fill my lips with happy shouting and my mouth with laughter. Let me see the HUMOR.

When was the last time you had a really good laugh? Let laughter lighten the load a little bit. Instead of dwelling always on the hard things, give yourself over to a merry heart with the Father. His sense of humor will always satisfy!

SHINE BRIGHTLY

*Those who are wise will shine like the brightness
on the horizon. Those who lead many people to
righteousness will shine like the stars forever and ever.*

DANIEL 12:3, GW

I name this day SHINE BRIGHTLY. I seek wisdom. I cultivate her with great respect and she serves me well. I live my life transparently, being real with my walk of faith. I'm open when I stumble and authentic when I find victory, too. In this way, I lead others to righteousness, and God promises me I will shine like the stars forever and ever.

Because I embrace wisdom, God causes me to SHINE BRIGHTLY.

Do you feel dim or do you feel radiant? I often meditate on the wisdom books in the Bible (Job, Psalms, Proverbs, Ecclesiastes, and Song of Solomon). These fortify me with the wisdom that comes from God. Whenever I look to Him I am radiant. That brilliance draws people to the God who lives in me.

SUBMIT TO THE STRETCH

*Do you remember how, on a racing-track,
every competitor runs, but only one wins the prize?
Well, you ought to run with your minds fixed on winning
the prize! Every competitor in athletic events goes
into serious training. Athletes will take tremendous
pains—for a fading crown of leaves. But our contest
is for an eternal crown that will never fade.*

1 CORINTHIANS 9:24-25, PHILLIPS

I name this day SUBMIT TO THE STRETCH. If I try to run a race before I stretch, my performance suffers. I could be injured or not even finish at all.

The same holds true with my destiny. If I try to run my race before I allow God to really stretch me, my performance suffers. The burn and discomfort I experience in my character now will keep me conditioned and able to cross the finish line. I will break the tape running at full stride if I SUBMIT TO THE STRETCH.

It is one thing to believe that God will work all things for your good. It is quite another to trust Him while He does it. Being stretched by obstacles, challenges, and adversity is not fun. But resistance builds strength. Trust that God has good things in store for you and be willing to humbly submit to His stretching.

OPENER OF DOORS

*As each has received a gift, use it to serve one
another, as good stewards of God's varied grace.*

1 PETER 4:10, ESV

I name this day OPENER OF DOORS. I am never small when I am making others great. I am a connector. I use my gifts to serve others. Like Abraham, I am blessed to be a blessing and through me, others are blessed.

Today I will provide for the success of others and help them fulfill their dreams. I know when I am a reservoir from which people can access my wisdom and expertise, I always find divine connections and encounter rich opportunities. I am an OPENER OF DOORS.

Look for opportunities to be a blessing today. Be on the alert and become a connector who links people together and creates opportunities. Put your gifts and skills to work for others and let God work through you.

CHERISHED

Love one another with brotherly affection.
Outdo one another in showing honor.

ROMANS 12:10, ESV

I name this day CHERISHED. I practice self-awareness and establish my priorities. I will tend to people and things which I highly value. I will pay attention to them and hold them in high regard and great esteem.

I will make time for what matters. I will not allow urgent things to cause me to push aside that which is important. I walk in honor. I am grateful for those God has placed in my life. I will make tangible my appreciation for them and will diligently communicate to those in my care that they are CHERISHED.

What is most important in your life? Who matters to you? Do your daily activities reflect that they are your priority? Note those you love well and create opportunities to let them know their value.

PERMANENT PROMISES

*Whatever God has promised gets stamped with the
Yes of Jesus. In Him, this is what we preach and pray,
the great Amen, God's Yes and our Yes together,
gloriously evident. God affirms us, making us a sure
thing in Christ, putting His Yes within us. By His Spirit
He has stamped us with His eternal pledge—a sure
beginning of what He is destined to complete.*

2 CORINTHIANS 1:20, MSG

I name this day PERMANENT PROMISES. My circumstances are temporary, but God's promises are eternal. My world is ever-changing, but He changes not.

I choose what I come into agreement with, so I choose to agree with God. My words come from my thoughts, and I believe what I hear myself repeatedly say. I align myself with what I declare. The truth I agree with trumps facts I experience. Today, I recognize and step into God's PERMANENT PROMISES.

When we get caught in a loop of negative thinking, there never seems to be a shortage of facts to convince us of how unfair things are. But this kind of thinking turns you into a victim and keeps you from accessing God's promises. What circumstances do you need to confront with the truth of God's Word today?

TRADITION

Now I commend you because you remember
Me in everything and maintain the traditions
even as I delivered them to you.

1 CORINTHIANS 11:2, ESV

I name this day TRADITION. I love things which link me to those who have gone before me. I honor memories, I maintain their values, and I preserve my heritage.

I want no part of legalistic rules which bind me to dead traditions. However, customs that hold me and my family together, impart strength, and guide my future by learning from the past—these I want to continue. These practices stabilize tomorrow by connecting me to yesterday. I get to choose those I will maintain and those I will let go. I have the power to create brand new ones that will be meaningful for generations to come. I thank God for the gift of story and memory and TRADITION.

There is value in connecting the past to the future, whether you are the first generation to begin, or the tenth to continue. What traditions hold meaning for you? What traditions would you like to begin?

SHEER GIFT

Consider it a sheer gift, friends, when tests and challenges come at you from all sides. You know that under pressure, your faith-life is forced into the open and shows its true colors. So don't try to get out of anything prematurely. Let it do its work so you become mature and well-developed, not deficient in any way.

JAMES 1:2-4, MSG

I name this day SHEER GIFT. Challenges are a gift. Problems are opportunities. Perseverance is part of the process to succeed.

Today, I speak blessings over seeds I have sown, over actions I have taken, and habits I have carefully developed. I will not give up or be discouraged. I press toward the mark for the high calling's prize. I will stay the course and allow the pressure of adversity to have its work. I will persist for the fruitful promise that is the reward of patience. Instead of complaining, I will embrace hard things and view them as a SHEER GIFT.

What is challenging you in this season? Consider this: without Goliath, David would have remained just a kid with some rocks in his pocket. Take a moment to thank God for the things which test your faith and produce endurance in you.

ASK BOLDLY

If you don't know what you're doing, pray to the
Father. He loves to help. You'll get His help, and won't
be condescended to when you ask for it. Ask boldly,
believingly, without a second thought. People who
"worry their prayers" are like wind-whipped waves.
Don't think you're going to get anything from the Master
that way, adrift at sea, keeping all your options open.

JAMES 1:5-8, MSG

I name this day ASK BOLDLY. I don't always know what to do. Though I search, I don't always find an obvious answer to my specific situation within the pages of scripture. So, I turn to You, Father, and ask You to help me. Guide me in uncertainty. Show me the next right thing.

I won't keep waffling between this or that, and I won't defer making decisions until I run out of options. No, I want to move forward and I am not afraid to ASK BOLDLY for Your help.

Sometimes we feel uncomfortable asking God for help—almost embarrassed that we don't already know what to do, or that what we need doesn't seem spiritual enough to bother Him about. He doesn't mind. He loves when you come boldly to Him and ask for His help. Ask now.

EXPECTATION

*... and all these blessings shall come upon you and overtake
you, because you obey the voice of the Lord your God:
Blessed shall you be in the city, and
blessed shall you be in the country.
Blessed shall be the fruit of your body, the produce
of your ground and the increase of your herds, the
increase of your cattle and the offspring of your flocks.
Blessed shall be your basket and your kneading bowl.
Blessed shall you be when you come in, and
blessed shall you be when you go out.*

DEUTERONOMY 28:2-6, NKJV

I name this day EXPECTATION. My expectations are like a magnet. They attract to me whatever I look for.

Therefore, I will expect on purpose—with intentionality. I won't let my expectations become established without my permission. I will set them.

Today, I expect favor. I expect divine appointments, revelation, insight, blessings, opportunities, laughter, joy, right timing, and extreme love. I create the world I want to live in through my EXPECTATION.

Do you expect good things to happen to you or are you always waiting for the other shoe to drop? Write down your blessings and make a gratitude list. Then, set your expectations to experience God's goodness. Look for blessings to overtake you. Expect it!

THINK WELL

Guard your heart more than anything else,
because the source of your life flows from it.

PROVERBS 4:23, GW

I name this day THINK WELL. I will eliminate "shrinking thinking" that causes me to pull back from opportunities because I fear failure or embarrassment.

My thoughts inform my actions, and my actions become my outcomes. Therefore, I will pay attention to my inner dialogue, I will guard my heart above all else and be careful to THINK WELL.

What do you tell yourself about yourself? Pay attention to your self-talk and you will soon find the root cause of your success or failure. Note negative thoughts so that you can replace them with the opposite, positive thought. Commit today to thinking well.

PURPOSE

*For which of you, desiring to build a tower, does
not first sit down and count the cost, whether he
has enough to complete it? Otherwise, when he
has laid a foundation and is not able to finish, all
who see it begin to mock him, saying, "This man
began to build and was not able to finish."*

LUKE 14:28-30, ESV

I name this day PURPOSE. I will keep my purpose before my eyes. I will remember my "why," and take charge of my time, energy, and resources so they are not diluted by things that take me outside my highest and best calling. I want to finish what I begin, and I want to finish well.

The social landscape is crowded with a myriad of options in which to engage. I can feel stretched out and tired just from considering my calendar. God, help me to count the cost of even my small decisions. I will remember to set my boundaries by first pushing every opportunity through the grid of PURPOSE.

Your community, your family, your church, job commitments, and other responsibilities compete for your energy, focus, and resources. Good is the enemy of better, better the enemy of best. Survey your calendar. If you push your priorities through the grid of purpose, what should go and what should remain?

APRIL

"And I will do whatever you ask in My name, so that the Father may be glorified in the Son. You may ask Me for anything in My name, and I will do it."

JOHN 14:13-14, NIV

MY EYES ARE UPON YOU

*O our God, will You not judge them? For we have no power
against this great multitude that is coming against us;
nor do we know what to do, but our eyes are upon You.*

2 CHRONICLES 20:12, NKJV

I name this day MY EYES ARE UPON YOU. Even when pain twists my heart with doubt, fear, and regret, when I am powerless against their attack and I don't know what to do, You are there.

You will judge the enemy. You will be my advocate in the courts of heaven. I look to the hills from whence cometh my help; O Lord, MY EYES ARE ON YOU.

Through everything you will ever endure, God will always rush to your aid. He is FOR you, not AGAINST you! All that He asks in return is for your EYES to be fixed on Him alone. In times of distress, where do you find your eyes?

APRIL 2

STEAL AWAY

*But when you pray, go into your room and shut the
door and pray to your Father who is in secret.
And your Father who sees in secret will reward you.*

MATTHEW 6:6, ESV

I name this day STEAL AWAY. I long for precious moments alone with God, away from others, free from tasks. Today I'll find a quiet place, shut away the world, and be with You. Because my heart longs for Your company, I will STEAL AWAY.

The world is filled with business, bustling, and boisterousness. Having a secret, quiet place, then, is seemingly counter-cultural. Even still, I encourage you to make room for seclusion. Use the quietness to talk, dream, and pray with the Father.

FOUND

*You will seek Me and find Me when you
seek Me with all your heart.*

JEREMIAH 29:13, NIV

I name this day FOUND. I am overwhelmed by the thought of the price You paid for me. I was lost, far away from You, destitute in my sin and shame, but You came and rescued me.

Therefore, I will seek You. I will seek peace and pursue it. I will step into joy, embrace hope, and enter Your rest. Oh the joy of knowing I once was lost but now have been FOUND!

One of the most beautiful things God has done is leave the ninety-nine for the one—that "one" being you. Amazing grace, indeed! Take time today to both celebrate being found and to press in, seeking to know Him more and more.

ACKNOWLEDGE

If anyone acknowledges that Jesus is the Son of
God, God lives in them and they in God.

1 JOHN 4:15, NIV

I name this day ACKNOWLEDGE. I acknowledge that God is the Father, that His Son is Jesus—veiled in flesh, crucified, risen, now at God's right hand—and that the Holy Spirit has come to comfort, instruct, and point me to Jesus. I acknowledge the wonder of the Trinity—heaven's great mystery, earth's great hope, and my heart's great joy.

Like Spurgeon, the overflow of the Triune love causes me to see "traces of the Trinity in every act of grace." This, I humbly ACKNOWLEDGE.

Acknowledging the Trinity wholeheartedly is crucial to accepting the Gospel. Are you allowing God to take up residence in your being? Where in your life do you still need to acknowledge the Godhead and allow the Triune being to fill you?

YEARNS FOR THEE

My soul yearns for You in the night;
in the morning my spirit longs for You.

ISAIAH 26:9a, NIV

I name this day YEARNS FOR THEE.

In the stillness of the night,

when I awake at morning's light;

in the busiest middle of the day,

in quietness as I stop to pray;

Oh, may it always and forever be,

that my heart and soul still YEARNS FOR THEE!

We often yearn for God in either of two scenarios: when all is well, or when all is crumbling. But do you yearn for Him in the middle? In the mundane? In the "everydayness" of an average afternoon? Stoke the embers of your soul with yearning!

STAY WITH IT

*"Stay with it—that's what is required.
Stay with it to the end.
You won't be sorry; you'll be saved."*

MARK 13:13, MSG

I name this day STAY WITH IT. Even when I grow weary, even when it is hard. When I am at the end of my capacity, I open my heart and believe God will enlarge and fill me. He will perfect that which concerns me. My portion is to STAY WITH IT.

When things grow difficult, it is tempting to throw in the towel, to sit the rest of this race out. But God has called you to run the race before you. What obstacles in your life feel insurmountable? Hand them to God and stay with it!

IN STEP

*Let the peace of Christ keep you in tune with
each other, in step with each other. None of
this going off and doing your own thing.*

COLOSSIANS 3:15, MSG

I name this day IN STEP. May God's peace envelope me in heaven's melody and cause me to walk in heaven's rhythm. No grand solos for me, I don't need to hear the sound of my own voice above the choir. Instead, may I join the great and mighty chorus. I want to sing the song in harmony and dance the choreography with others, beautifully IN STEP.

You've heard the phrase, "There's no 'I' in TEAM," but did you know that this phrase has biblical roots? Are you living in step with others, or do you tend to go it alone? He is a God of family, tribes, and nations. You were born to belong!

ENCOUNTER

*God did this so that they would seek Him
and perhaps reach out for Him and find Him,
though He is not far from any one of us.*

ACTS 17:27, NIV

I name this day ENCOUNTER. Today I seek a purposeful encounter with the Almighty. I seek Him, in the hopes that I may feel my way toward Him and find Him, knowing He is never actually far from me, no matter how I feel.

One moment—just one moment—changes everything! One moment in His presence can right wrongs, mend broken things, settle injustice, and give me a glimpse of glory divine. Oh, that I may know Him and be known by Him! May I not seek His hand more than His face. Today, my heart's desire is a purposeful ENCOUNTER.

One moment with God can change a lifetime of mistakes made and consequences endured without Him. You have access to such power right now! When was the last true encounter you experienced with God? This can happen daily, you just have to reach out to Him.

DISCOVER

It is the glory of God to conceal a matter,
but the glory of kings is to search out a matter.

PROVERBS 25:2, NASB

I name this day DISCOVER. I am searching out the deep matters—this is the glory of kings! Because I am a king and a priest, to me it has been given to know the secrets of the kingdom of heaven.

Today, I am on a quest of discovery to seek out heaven's treasures. I long to know the riches of wisdom available in God's Word and search out the understanding that increases my comprehension and ability to apply wisdom. I ask, seek, and knock, therefore, I will DISCOVER.

Have you ever prepared a treasure hunt for a child? It is great fun to watch them search for gifts you have hidden for them to find. When you are curious, ask questions, and seek to know more, it gives God this same kind of joy!

GOD'S ENERGY

Be energetic in your life of salvation, reverent and sensitive before God. That energy is God's energy, an energy deep within you, God Himself willing and working at what will give Him the most pleasure.

PHILIPPIANS 2:13, MSG

I name this day GOD'S ENERGY. God Himself lives in me, and He is willing and working at what gives Him the most pleasure.

When I am yielded to the Father, my endeavors are fueled by GOD'S ENERGY.

Let God's Spirit living in you bubble up and spill out onto everything you do today! His energy is within you. He can refresh and restore you. Revive and revitalize you. He is working for your good, and this brings Him great pleasure!

WHAT CAN'T BE BOUGHT

You're blessed when you're content with just who you are—
no more, no less. That's the moment you find yourselves
proud owners of everything that can't be bought.

MATTHEW 5:5, MSG

I name this day WHAT CAN'T BE BOUGHT. I have humble gratitude for that which has built my character, shaped my identity, and fashioned who I am. Every gift, every blessing, every trial has given to me WHAT CAN'T BE BOUGHT.

Material items will fade away. What will last are the God-given treasures within you. What you have endured has inevitably made you into who you are—the image of God reflected within you. Are you bearing the image or trying to change it?

FAMILY

If one part suffers, every part suffers with it;
if one part is honored every part rejoices with it.

1 CORINTHIANS 12:26, NIV

I name this day FAMILY—the covenant kind. I am grateful for those I call family, whether by blood relation or chosen by choice. These are the ones for whom I willingly sacrifice, will lay down my life, in honor prefer, weep with, laugh with, stand with, and pray for. Thank You, God for relationships that matter. Thank You that I am part of a FAMILY.

Family—the highest call, the deepest sacrifice, the greatest reward. True family, by blood, marriage, or deep friendship, is about doing life together, developing relationships that matter. What relationships matter to you? Celebrate these today.

ALL-GENEROUS IN LOVE

For God is sheer beauty, all-generous
in love, loyal always and ever.

PSALM 100:5, MSG

I name this day ALL-GENEROUS IN LOVE. Because I am born of God, I have a noble origin. Because I am loved liberally by my Father, I can be liberal in giving love.

My heart is overflowing with God's light, love, and beauty. Therefore, I have a bountiful supply which affords me the great privilege to be ALL-GENEROUS IN LOVE.

God's never-ending, forever-sufficient love flows through your veins. Because you are an heir to His throne, you will never run out! Who are you sharing His love with? How can you better be all-generous in demonstrating God's love to others?

FAITHFUL GOD

*Understand, therefore, that the Lord your God is indeed
God. He is the faithful God who keeps His covenant for
a thousand generations and lavishes His unfailing love
on those who love Him and obey His commands.*

DEUTERONOMY 7:9, NLT

I name this day FAITHFUL GOD. He keeps His covenants and fulfills His promises. He holds me in the palm of His hand, defends me against every foe, and delights in me.

When all else around me fails, when men disappoint me and fail to keep their covenants, I rejoice that I am subject to a FAITHFUL GOD.

God has never forsaken you or left you dry—He is ever-faithful to His children. What are you still believing for Him to bring you through? Meditate today on His faithfulness and let this fill you with comfort and hope.

REMEMBER

But then I recall all You have done, O LORD;
I remember Your wonderful deeds of long ago.

PSALM 77:11, NLT

I name this day REMEMBER. I will look back and recount the blessings of God—promises fulfilled, faithfulness proven, kindness made known. What He has done before, He can do again. Therefore, I will keep hope alive, kindled afresh because I REMEMBER.

There will never come a time when His promise leaves you unfulfilled. What has God brought you through in times past? What victories can you recall? Today, remember the battles and celebrate the victories. He did it before and will do it again.

WITNESS

*I am praying not only for them but also for those who
believe in Me because of them and their witness about Me.*

JOHN 17:20, MSG

I name this day WITNESS. Jesus talks to the Father about me—
which blows my mind! May my words and actions testify well of
His faithfulness and my allegiance. Jesus prays for me. Incredible!

Not only does He pray for me, He intercedes for those who will
come to believe in Him because of my WITNESS.

---

*You, dear child, are always on God's mind! He is always looking for
ways to grow you, to better you, and to pour His love out on you. Where
can you be an intentional witness for Him? In what ways can you allow
your life to reveal more of His glory?*

REVEALED TRUTH

*The Friend, the Holy Spirit whom the Father will
send at My request, will make everything plain
to you. He will remind you of all the things I have
told you. I'm leaving you well and whole.*

JOHN 14:26-27, MSG

I name this day REVEALED TRUTH. Oh, what joy when God shares something with me I have not before seen. How excited I get when I discover things not taught to me by man but shown to me by His Spirit! The heavens open, mysteries come into the light, and my soul rejoices at the wonder of REVEALED TRUTH!

The Holy Spirit loves to reveal His beauty and kindness to His children. All is made well and whole, and through His revealed truth, we lack nothing! Ask Him to show you something you have never before seen. Ask Him to reveal truth to you today.

STEADFAST

*Therefore, my beloved brothers, be steadfast,
immovable, always abounding in the work of the Lord,
knowing that in the Lord your labor is not in vain.*

1 CORINTHIANS 15:58, ESV

I name this day STEADFAST. Let the words of my mouth and the meditation of my heart be acceptable in Thy sight. Help me to be immovable and know that my labor is not in vain. May I be loyal and always abounding in the Word of God. Anchored to the Rock, I am STEADFAST.

If your foundation is on the Rock, you will never be shaken. Where are you struggling to remain steadfast? Upon what is your foundation built? Meditate on the fundamentals and shore up your foundations.

COMPLETELY DEPENDABLE

The One who called you is completely
dependable. If He said it, He'll do it!

1 THESSALONIANS 5:24, MSG

I name this day COMPLETELY DEPENDABLE. Knowing God is this to me brings such peace. Reaching to grasp His sovereignty opens my spirit to enjoy greater trust and renewed hope. I rest in releasing the outcomes knowing God is COMPLETELY DEPENDABLE.

Rest in this promise: Jehovah Jireh, the Provider, will meet every need within you, and then leave your cup overflowing. What area of your life do you need to trust Him most? What do you need to release into His care?

ABOUND IN HOPE

So because our hope is set on what is yet to be seen,
we patiently keep on waiting for its fulfillment.

ROMANS 8:25, TPT

I name this day ABOUND IN HOPE. As I trust and believe, may God fill me with joy and peace. His hope anchors my soul when turbulent storms rage around me. His hope lights my path when darkness obscures my vision.

I will wait patiently for the fulfillment of things I have handed to You, God. Through the power of the Holy Spirit at work in me, I will ABOUND IN HOPE.

In every season, God will fill you with the joy to make it through, the hope to move forward, and the peace to be still through it all. Beneath the shadow of His wings, you will always abound in hope.

OVERFLOW

*Thou preparest a table before me in the
presence of mine enemies: Thou anointest
my head with oil; my cup runneth over.*

PSALM 23:5, KJV

I name this day OVERFLOW. Because You anoint my head with oil,
my cup overflows.

I walk in the power of Your anointing. It gives me the permission
to handle Your glory and the courage to trust Your grace. Today,
I decree an overflow of the anointing, an overflow of mercy and
grace, an overflow of provision. In every good and perfect thing, I
give thanks for God's OVERFLOW.

---

*Are you aware of God's anointing on your life? Do you understand your
authority as a believer? You are not an orphan, not a child of lack. You are
God's chosen one to whom He pours out His wildest affection and desires
for you to live in the overflow.*

APRIL 22

UPGRADE

*But You'll welcome us with open arms when we run
for cover to You. Let the party last all night! Stand
guard over our celebration. You are famous, God, for
welcoming God-seekers, for decking us out in delight.*

PSALM 5:11-12, MSG

I name this day UPGRADE! It is time to step into priority access and experience all the riches of God's favor and blessing.

U—Unparalleled Favor

P—Premium Opportunities

G—Glorious Encounters

R—Rained Down Blessings

A—Adventures in the Anointing

D—Daily Miracles

E—Ever-increasing Insights and Revelation

I decree that today is a day of UPGRADE!

Are you ready for an upgrade? I challenge you to step into the flow of God's favor today. He delights in you! Let yourself believe He enjoys lavishing you with His love. Enjoy loving Him and celebrate His goodness today.

LIGHT

*For at one time you were darkness, but now you
are light in the Lord. Walk as children of light.*

EPHESIANS 5:8, ESV

I name this day LIGHT. It overcomes darkness. It pushes back shadows as it radiates hope and comfort and joy.

I decree illumination today—light for my path. More than that, may the light of Christ be reflected in me so brightly that others may see its glow and bask in the warmth. I have clarity and my steps are ordered because I am a child of LIGHT.

Take notice of light today everywhere you go. Pay attention to the contrast of shadow and light, the warmth and brightness of the sun, the flicker of a candle's flame. You are drawn to light because you are a child of light. Shine brightly.

DIRECTION

The steps of a [good and righteous] man are directed and established by the Lord, and He delights in his way [and blesses his path].

PSALM 37:23, AMP

I name this day DIRECTION. The Lord orders my steps. His Word is a lamp for my feet and a light for my path.

I come against all confusion and indecision today. I will trust my gut. I will rely on the Holy Spirit to bear witness within me and make God's highest and best known, even when I cannot see the big picture and do not have all the details. May He who knows the end from the beginning provide me with clear DIRECTION.

When we are unsure of what to do, it is easy to become paralyzed with indecision. Endlessly weighing all the options and fearing to take a wrong step, we take no steps. But you have the Holy Spirit as your guide. Take a step today, trusting His direction.

BLESSING

*The angel of God spoke from Heaven a second time to
Abraham: "I swear—God's sure word!—because you
have gone through with this, and have not refused to
give me your son, your dear, dear son, I'll bless you—
oh, how I'll bless you! And I'll make sure that your
children flourish—like stars in the sky! Like sand on
the beaches! And your descendants will defeat their
enemies. All nations on Earth will find themselves blessed
through your descendants because you obeyed Me."*

GENESIS 22:15-18, MSG

I name this day BLESSING. The breakthrough I am seeking may be escorted in by the blessing I become for someone else.

I will shift my focus past my need, look beyond survival of this moment, and become somebody's miracle. I walk in obedience, therefore I am blessed and I will be a BLESSING!

Ask God to highlight someone to you today to whom you can be a blessing. Maybe you will speak a word of encouragement, pick up the tab for a stranger, leave a large tip, perform a task for a neighbor ... Become a tangible blessing today.

AUTHENTIC EXPRESSION

Do not lie to one another, since you have put off
the old man with his deeds, and have put on the
new man who is renewed in knowledge according
to the image of Him who created him.

COLOSSIANS 3:9-10, NKJV

I name this day AUTHENTIC EXPRESSION—it is a beautiful thing, my gift to the world, my gift to the King! I honor Him when my words and deeds are congruent with His nature in me. The One who formed me in my mother's womb and equipped me with my personality and abilities created me in His image.

I want His image to shine through me unhindered, no mask, no veil of pretense or make-believe. I commit to living my life as an AUTHENTIC EXPRESSION of Christ in me.

Our old nature wears a mask and works to be accepted and liked.
Sometimes, we act in ways that are not congruent with the new nature
of Christ alive in us. In what areas do you need to exhibit a more authentic
expression of who you are in Jesus?

ANTICIPATION

*Faith assures us of things we expect and convinces
us of the existence of things we cannot see.*

HEBREWS 11:1, GW

I name this day ANTICIPATION. Looking forward to what is to come gives me joy. It opens my heart and mind to incredible possibilities and lets me dream crazy dreams.

God delights in fulfilling—in exceeding—my expectations. Today, I open myself up to new levels of faith and new expressions of joy. I will release my inner child and let my imagination come out to play. I won't be locked down, believing for only that which I can see. I believe. I expect, I step into blissful ANTICIPATION!

Have you lost your sense of wonder? Is there anything you look forward to with as much delight as a young child awaiting Christmas morning? Ask God to kindle anticipation within you. Play. Use your imagination and spark some joy!

AFFIRMATION

Don't say anything that would hurt another person. Instead, speak only what is good so that you can give help wherever it is needed. That way, what you say will help those who hear you.

EPHESIANS 4:29, GW

I name this day AFFIRMATION. I will take encouragement from wherever it comes. I will allow the smallest breath of affirmation to rekindle the dormant embers of my soul and lift me.

I will give encouragement wherever I can, noticing others with the eyes of heaven. I will be intentional to lift others, a gift within my power to grant. Father, let me see what you see and be faithful to speak words of AFFIRMATION.

Affirming others is a wonderful habit to develop. Heighten your awareness as you move about your day and speak kind words of blessing to those you encounter. Elevate, encourage, and lift others everywhere you go.

FOCUS

Let your eyes look straight ahead;
fix your gaze directly before you.

PROVERBS 4:25, NIV

I name this day FOCUS. By focusing on less, I achieve more. Help me to focus on what matters and let the rest go. I fix my gaze straight ahead.

I will be intentional with my focus today, and not allow distractions and the priorities of others to pull me off course. I decree laser-like clarity over my thoughts and declare incremental improvement over all my endeavors. I strengthen my power by increasing my FOCUS.

What is distracting you from accomplishing the things that most matter? Write down where you need to concentrate your focus and keep this with you throughout your day. Commit this work to the Lord. Ask for His focus in this area.

RESONANCE

*And above all these put on love, which binds
everything together in perfect harmony.*

COLOSSIANS 3:14, ESV

I name this day RESONANCE. As a tuning fork vibrates to the resonant frequency of its design, may I vibrate to heaven's frequency, in perfect pitch with God's design.

I decree harmony today. I declare that the sound coming forth from my spirit, the meditation of my heart, and the words in my mouth all vibrate to the frequency of my Creator, well tuned and in perfect RESONANCE.

There is such beauty in a symphony. When an orchestra plays, all their individual sounds come together for a glorious expression of the composer's vision. Ask God to help you be in tune with heaven and blend your voice with others in holy unity.

MAY

Shout with joy to the Lord, all the earth!
Worship the Lord with gladness.
Come before Him, singing with joy.
Acknowledge that the Lord is God!
He made us, and we are His.
We are His people, the sheep of His pasture.
Enter His gates with thanksgiving;
go into His courts with praise.
Give thanks to Him and praise His name.
For the Lord is good.
His unfailing love continues forever,
and His faithfulness continues to each generation.

PSALM 100:1-5, NLT

HE FIRST LOVED ME

We love because He first loved us.

1 JOHN 4:19, NIV

I name this day HE FIRST LOVED ME. That love is my fuel. My rescue. My redemption. In gratitude for the love shown me, in worship of the One who plucked me from death, willingly I turn my heart towards mankind. Any goodness, servanthood, or compassion found in my heart is because HE FIRST LOVED ME.

He first loved you so that you could show His love to all of mankind! It can sometimes feel difficult to bear witness to His character, especially to those who need it most. Why do you think this is? Where are you sharing His goodness and His love today?

IN THE KNOWLEDGE OF HIM

Grace and peace be yours in abundance through the
knowledge of God and of Jesus our Lord.
His divine power has given us everything we need
for a godly life through our knowledge of Him
who called us by His own glory and goodness.

2 PETER 1:2-3, NIV

I name this day IN THE KNOWLEDGE OF HIM. I can know only what You reveal, see only what You shows me, understand only what You explain. My prayer today is that the eyes of my heart might be opened, that in searching the corners of my imagination, I might be set ablaze with passion IN THE KNOWLEDGE OF HIM.

What has God emblazoned upon your heart in this season? Whatever that may be, take a moment to dream alongside God about it. What is He revealing to you? As you partner with God, He will plant His knowledge in you!

WISELY AND WELL

Oh! Teach us to live well!
Teach us to live wisely and well!

PSALM 90:12, MSG

I name this day WISELY and WELL. This is my heart's desire; to prosper and be in good health as my soul prospers.

I will nurture my soul's health today, feeding it with things that fill my tank emotionally and spiritually. I will walk in the fear of the Lord and pursue the wisdom of God that comes from meditating upon His Word. Teach me, Oh God, to live WISELY and WELL.

What does "living well" mean to you? What feeds your soul? What nurtures your spirit? Though you might be encouraged to answer this through a worldly lens, dig a little deeper. Let the wisdom of God train you how to prosper in all things.

ENCOURAGEMENT

For whatever was written in the past was written for our instruction, so that we may have hope through endurance and through the encouragement from the Scriptures.

ROMANS 15:4, CSB

I name this day ENCOURAGEMENT. Only through the hope of restoration and the promise of life renewed can I continue to press toward the mark. When my soul is downcast, I must rehearse past victories to strengthen my faith and resolve.

I will build myself up today by speaking words of life over my dreams. I will stir up the gifts that are within me by rehearsing the promises of God over my life. My endurance is made possible because I have found this ENCOURAGEMENT.

The ultimate encouragement as a believer is this: you have been cleansed in Christ's blood. Jesus has breathed new life into you. Take refuge in His promises today. Savor the Word of God—it's where you will find encouragement to endure.

INVENTIVE

So let's do it—full of belief, confident that we're presentable inside and out. Let's keep a firm grip on the promises that keep us going. He always keeps His word. Let's see how inventive we can be in encouraging love and helping out, not avoiding worshiping together as some do but spurring each other on, especially as we see the big day approaching.

HEBREWS 10:24-25, MSG

I name this day INVENTIVE. I have a firm grip on God's promises and I am presentable to Him because Christ is in me. Today let encouragement pour out of me, may love spring forth from me to others, spurring them on in ways which are INVENTIVE.

Finding new avenues to lend a helping hand to others can feel intimidating, but God has implanted creativity within you for such a time as this! You are creative and resourceful. How can you make a difference today in a new and inventive way?

INFLUENCE

*You are the salt of the earth, but if salt has lost
its taste, how shall its saltiness be restored? It is
no longer good for anything except to be thrown
out and trampled under people's feet.
You are the light of the world. A city set on a hill cannot
be hidden. Nor do people light a lamp and put it under a
basket, but on a stand, and it gives light to all in the house.
In the same way, let your light shine before
others, so that they may see your good works and
give glory to your Father who is in heaven.*

MATTHEW 5:13-16, ESV

I name this day INFLUENCE. I am a world changer, the world does not change me. I will use my influence under His influence.

I decree that my influence today will be positive. I am salt. I am light. I carry hope and I bring joy. I want what is inside me to be so fragrant and attractive that others want what I've got. I will intentionally steward my INFLUENCE.

God has given you authority and dominion—influence—over your corner of the world. If you never use it, however, it's useless! Are you stewarding your influence? If not, in what ways can you begin to leverage your influence to bring God glory?

PRIVILEGE

Taste and see that the Lord is good.
Oh, the joys of those who take refuge in Him!

PSALM 34:8, NLT

I name this day PRIVILEGE. It is such a privilege to be alive! Every breath, every heartbeat, every moment—I take none of it for granted.

Today I will be actively grateful. I will count every blessing, complain about nothing, and find joy in things great and small. I set my mind on the goodness of God. That I am His and loved by Him is an awesome PRIVILEGE.

It can be easy to take it all, big or small, for granted at times. But, as the tried-and-true hymn goes, "Come, thou fount of ev'ry blessing, tune my heart to sing Thy grace." Let this be your prayer: "Lord, tune my heart to sing Your grace today."

PREPARED

Be prepared. You're up against far more than you can handle on your own. Take all the help you can get, every weapon God has issued, so that when it's all over but the shouting, you'll still be on your feet.

EPHESIANS 6:13, MSG

I name this day PREPARED. Humbly, gratefully I accept tools, weapons, and training. On my own, I am in totally over my head. I need the power of God and wisdom of heaven. Through faith and practice, I am PREPARED.

Going it alone will leave you vulnerable, susceptible to attack. God has equipped you so that you will be able to stay standing tall as the enemy falls to the left and right of you. What are some areas you feel are being left open to attack? What scriptures can you stand on to fortify your soul's preparation?

FIGHT

For we do not wrestle against flesh and blood, but against the rulers, against the authorities, against the cosmic powers over this present darkness, against the spiritual forces of evil in the heavenly places. Therefore take up the whole armor of God, that you may be able to withstand in the evil day, and having done all, to stand firm.

EPHESIANS 6:12-13, ESV

I name this day FIGHT. I will fight for things that matter. I will contend for what I care about.

Today I yield no ground to the enemy. I do not acquiesce. I do not allow negative thoughts to pollute my mind nor negative people to control my atmosphere. I float like a butterfly and sting like a bee, I stand up to the enemy, I do not flee! Today, I am fit for FIGHT!

Even when the war feels stacked against you, God has given you His armor so that you are protected from the enemy's blows. What battle are you fighting today? You are fit for the fight. Rise up!

RECOMPENSE

*God is just: He will pay back trouble
to those who trouble you.*

2 THESSALONIANS 1:6, NIV

I name this day RECOMPENSE. I rely on the justice of God. Even if a whole army surrounded me, I do not need to be afraid. He is my shield and buckler. He is my defender—a present help in time of trouble.

I decree no harm shall befall me. I declare angels are encamped about me and they surround my family. I decree double for our trouble (Isaiah 61:7). The enemy is subdued and his only authorized action toward me is RECOMPENSE!

RECOMPENSE: *compensation given
for loss or harm suffered.*

God has gone before you. He is fighting the battle alongside you and protecting you from harm. Today, rest in the truth of His promise to you that the enemy MUST flee at His name. He is a just God who fights on your behalf. What have you lost that requires recompense?

HEART OF THE MATTER

We justify our actions by appearances;
God examines our motives.

PROVERBS 21:2, MSG

I name this day HEART OF THE MATTER. I see only fruit, but God sees all the way to the root. He knows your every trial, every battle, every broken thing, every area of blame or shame.

I release the shame. Instead of walking in harsh judgment or bitter regret, God, help me discern the HEART OF THE MATTER.

In a world that points fingers, casts blame, and refuses to see beyond the surface, you have access to a God who sees the heart of the matter. In what areas do you need clearer discernment to get to the root issue causing you shame or blocking your victory? Ask. He'll answer.

TAKE HEART

"Here on earth you will have many trials and sorrows.
But take heart, because I have overcome the world."

JOHN 16:33, NLT

I name this day TAKE HEART. The thief which is determined to steal my joy, kill my hope, and destroy my life has a sure and certain fate. Any access he has is temporary. In the scope of eternity, any affliction from his hand is light and momentary.

My Redeemer lives in me and He has already overcome. Because of this joy that is set before me, because the favorable outcome is promised, because in God I can step into the finished work, I can TAKE HEART.

Jesus has answered every fear, every trouble, and every dark night with an empty tomb and scarred hands and feet. His sacrifice has unleashed pure, unbridled joy to you! Take heart—though your sorrow may last the night, joy cometh in the morning! Your victory is assured.

GIVEN REST

I name this day GIVEN REST. I come to Him with my burdens. When I choose to trust Him enough to lay them down and release the heavy load, He takes them from me.

He offers me a place to rest in His love. He brings me to an oasis of peace near His quiet brook of bliss. There in the kindness of His presence, weariness melts. He restores and revives my life as I am GIVEN REST.

Have you run yourself empty? Come and rest at His feet. Bring your tiredness, your hurt, your emptiness. Let Him refill you and melt away your exhaustion. He has given rest to you. Find time today to trust God enough to lay it down and accept the given rest from your Father.

UNSWERVING HOPE

*Let us hold unswervingly to the hope we
profess, for He who promised is faithful.*

HEBREWS 10:23, NIV

I name this day UNSWERVING HOPE. It is an anchor to my soul, it
is a buoy to my spirit, a life raft to my mind. Come what may, the
promises of God and the eternal restoration of all things creates in
me an UNSWERVING HOPE.

*God will never leave you lost at sea. His unswerving hope will always
bring you safely back to shore! In this season, where has your hope
run thin? What disappointments have blocked you from receiving and
walking in hope? Hand them to Jesus and let His hope fill your soul once
again.*

PORTAL TO GOD'S POWER

But He answered me, "My grace is always more than enough for you, and My power finds its full expression through your weakness." So I will celebrate my weaknesses, for when I'm weak I sense more deeply the mighty power of Christ living in me. So I'm not defeated by my weakness, but delighted! For when I feel my weakness and endure mistreatment—when I'm surrounded with troubles on every side and face persecution because of my love for Christ—I am made yet stronger. For my weakness becomes a portal to God's power.

2 CORINTHIANS 12:9-10, TPT

I name this day PORTAL TO GOD'S POWER. My weaknesses do not define me. They do not diminish me or disqualify me from God's service.

God, I surrender my shortcomings to You, today. Extend Your grace to me. Wrap around me like a corset and strengthen my spiritual spine. I confess my sin. I acknowledge my failure. I surrender these to You without shame because the blood of Jesus covers me. I can celebrate today because I am made stronger—my weaknesses have become a PORTAL TO GOD'S POWER.

You have an all-access pass to supernatural strength in all things— through God, all things are possible. When surrendered, your weaknesses become an avenue to stepping into God's strength. What do you need His strength to conquer today?

EXUBERANTLY BLESSED

And I command you today: Love God, your God.
Walk in His ways. Keep His commandments,
regulations, and rules so that you will live, really
live, live exuberantly, blessed by God, your God,
in the land you are about to enter and possess.

DEUTERONOMY 30:16, MSG

I name this day EXUBERANTLY BLESSED. That's how I want to live, guided by the covenant He has lovingly written on my heart. I enter the place of His promise only by grace. I possess the promise by surrender. I am loved. By God, I am EXUBERANTLY BLESSED.

When you walk in the guidance of God, you unlock abundant, exuberant blessing! What is guiding the way you live?

ABSOLUTELY

*And don't allow yourselves to be weary in
planting good seeds, for the season of reaping the
wonderful harvest you've planted is coming!*

GALATIANS 6:9, TPT

I name this day ABSOLUTELY. I will absolutely do what it takes. I will absolutely push through difficulties. I will absolutely not back down.

I place my trust in the One who is absolute. Forgetting what lies behind, I press toward the mark for the prize of the high calling of God in Christ Jesus. I decree perseverance today—strength in my body, mind, and soul. If my dreams are God-given and heaven-inspired, will I realize them? ABSOLUTELY!

There is no gray area in the character of God—He is always absolute. He is never-changing. What gray area are you struggling with? Where has doubt crept in? Bring this to God—He can handle it—ask for His absolute truth and the confidence this brings to be revealed to you today.

WONDERFULLY MADE

I praise You, for I am fearfully and wonderfully made.
Wonderful are Your works; my soul knows it very well.

PSALM 139:14, ESV

I name this day WONDERFULLY MADE. Everything God crafts is well made; what He designs is filled with beauty, order, purpose, and excellence.

Today I command my self image to align with the image of God in me. I decree my thoughts will agree with His thoughts toward me. I will honor Him by allowing my soul to declare His wonderful works. I am fearfully and WONDERFULLY MADE.

You have been created in the likeness of God. You are fashioned exactly as He wanted you to be. Anything that has marred or scarred you can be redeemed and restored by His precious blood. You are fully seen, fully known, and fully loved by your Creator. You are His masterpiece through and through!

HOLY

*Therefore, if anyone cleanses himself from what
is dishonorable, he will be a vessel for honorable
use, set apart as holy, useful to the master of
the house, ready for every good work.*

2 TIMOTHY 2:21, ESV

I name this day HOLY. I am a vessel of honor, an instrument set apart for special purposes, made holy, useful to the Master, and prepared to do any good work.

I consecrate myself today. I choose to lay my motives before the Lord and have Him search me and try me. I am full of flaws, but when I surrender and throw myself on His mercy, His righteousness makes me righteous. Because He is holy, I can be HOLY.

You are set apart—different in your composition, nature, and calling. You can never be holy on your own, you must step into the holiness of Jesus. He has reconciled you to God. When God looks at you, He sees Jesus. What must you surrender to align your heart to His holiness?

MATCHLESS

Give thanks to the LORD, for He is good.
His faithful love endures forever.

PSALM 136:1, CSB

I name this day MATCHLESS. The hymn goes, "How marvelous, how wonderful, and my song shall ever be; how marvelous, how wonderful is my Savior's love for me."

Today I intentionally step into God's glorious grace. I happily explore His fathomless depths. I decree my curiosity unleashed, may it roam the rooms of heaven. I run freely through His limitless space and know that He has given me every place my feet shall walk on. His worth is MATCHLESS!

Matchless worth, glorious grace,
fathomless depths, limitless space.

It's impossible to put a price tag on Christ's love for you—every good thing you have ever experienced is due to His handiwork. Position your mind to consider the works of His hands with curiosity and wonder. Free your mind to experience Him as matchless!

GOD'S TIMING

" ... for I am God, and there is no other;
I am God, and there is none like Me,
declaring the end from the beginning
and from ancient times things not yet done,
saying, 'My counsel shall stand,
and I will accomplish all My purpose ...'"

ISAIAH 46:9b-10, ESV

I name this day GOD'S TIMING. You know my end from the beginning and all the parts in between. Time, therefore is one of Your gifts, another expression of Your love. So when I am frustrated with a delay or feel like You have forgotten my prayer, when it seems You have missed opening a door, abandoned a promise, or left me coping with disappointment, I will remember that Your sovereignty includes the marking of time.

Your plans for me are good. Your love for me is attentive. Grant me the bouyancy of hope and the grace to trust GOD'S TIMING.

Is there something you or a loved one has been waiting and waiting for His answer or intervention? God has not forgotten. It has not escaped His notice. Hand this thing to Him today and ask for His grace to cover you. Ask for the faith you need to trust Him ... and His timing.

FOR MY GOOD

*So we are convinced that every detail of our lives is
continually woven together for good, for we are His lovers
who have been called to fulfill His designed purpose.*

ROMANS 8:28, TPT

I name this day FOR MY GOOD. What God has begun, He will be faithful to complete. It feels like a mess in the middle, too many loose ends to ever turn into tapestry. I resemble a mosaic of broken pieces far more than a painted canvas, but I trust the Artist—whatever His medium or method.

I yield to the process. He perfects that which concerns me, and all the things happening in my life, He is working FOR MY GOOD.

Sometimes it feels as though God has forgotten His promises. When the world is crashing down, or when hard things confront you, it can be hard to see (or believe) that God can (or will) work this for your good. Know this: God is at work. He will weave the details together for your good.

HOLD MY PEACE

The Lord will fight for you,
and you shall hold your peace.

EXODUS 14:14, NKJV

I name this day HOLD MY PEACE. Standing is mine to do. Resisting is mine to do. Fighting the battle is not. Telling God how to fight the battle is not. I need to keep my mouth shut.

Today I will trust God to fight for me. I won't fret, complain, struggle, or curse the situation. I will take comfort that the Lord fights for me and I will HOLD MY PEACE.

Our words are powerful, and what we release into the atmosphere has consequences. Murmering, complaining, sweating, and fretting keep us from standing in the place of victory. When tempted to commiserate, stop. Hold your peace and let the Lord fight your battle.

ESTABLISHED

Let the favor of the Lord our God be upon us,
and establish the work of our hands upon us;
yes, establish the work of our hands!

PSALM 90:17, ESV

I name this day ESTABLISHED. May God establish, decree by authority, ordain, and appoint the work of my hands.

May He settle, confirm, and ratify my authorized work. Let me walk in His favor. May my hands not waver or falter but fulfill and make good on the work which He has ESTABLISHED for me.

ESTABLISHED: *set up firmly, on a permanent basis; made true or certain.*

Is the work you do established by God? How can you know what work is authorized and ordained by Him for you? Ask Him. Ask God what He has created you for. Ask Him to reveal His purpose and establish the work of your hands.

PROCESS

The earth produces the crops on its own.
First a leaf blade pushes through, then the heads of
wheat are formed, and finally the grain ripens.

MARK 4:28, NLT

I name this day PROCESS. Everything that matures and bears fruit has patience as part of the recipe. Growth requires a process. Things have a beginning, a middle, and an end.

Today I embrace the natural unfolding of days and events that will lead me and those I love into maturity and fruitfulness. I will not rush. I will not force time. I will graciously, willingly, and joyfully embrace the PROCESS.

I hate process. I prefer to achieve my way through things—decree, declare, and move on. But that isn't always how it works. There is a process involved in being perfected. Salvation's process is sanctification. Where are you in your process? How can you honor the process and cooperate more fully?

SPRING FORTH

*Behold, the former things have come to
pass, and new things I now declare; before
they spring forth I tell you of them.*

ISAIAH 42:9, ESV

I name this day SPRING FORTH. No matter how far you have been pushed or buried, no matter how under it all you feel, it is only a season. You will soon break out with new life!

I decree strong roots are forming while you feel unseen. I declare you are growing when it looks like nothing is happening. This might feel like a setback, but it is a setup for your comeback. Newness is on the way. Great things are about to SPRING FORTH.

God loves to communicate with you. He loves to reveal Himself to your heart. Ask Him what He thinks of you. Ask Him what His favorite thing is about you. Ask Him what He is about to do in your life. Let Him declare newness to your heart today, and let hope spring forth.

OVERTURNED

*For the law of the Spirit of life has set you free in
Christ Jesus from the law of sin and death.*

ROMANS 8:2, ESV

I name this day OVERTURNED. Whatever has ruled against you, we break its power.

The principalities over this world are often revealed through systems of this world, like puppets on a string. Today I come against the enemy—and my enemy is not flesh and blood. I call upon my Advocate, Jesus, and step into the throne room of heaven and see that the verdict of the world's system squeezing my has been OVERTURNED!

The enemy of your soul comes against you with lies, distorting the truth until you waver and yield your victory. Sin and death have no hold on you. Christ, your redeemer, has pardoned you, He has reconciled you to the Father, and overturned the sentence of death. Live in freedom!

JUSTICE

He is the Rock, His works are perfect,
and all His ways are just.
A faithful God who does no wrong,
upright and just is He.

DEUTERONOMY 32:4, NIV

I name this day JUSTICE. Let the justice of God weight the scales and confirm that the outcome of heaven is manifested on earth.

I stand in the gap today. I step into the courts of heaven and make intercession for others. I declare righteousness will win the day. I decree mercy, compassion, and JUSTICE.

What causes stir in you the heart of justice? Who is voiceless that you can become a voice for? Step into the justice of God today. Intercede and act. Ask God to highlight to you areas in which you can stand in agreement with His justice today.

ABLE

Now to Him who is able to keep you from stumbling,
and to present you faultless before the presence
of His glory with exceeding joy, to God our Savior,
who alone is wise, be glory and majesty, dominion
and power, both now and forever. Amen.

JUDE 1:24-25, NKJV

I name this day ABLE. Because He is, I am.

It is not by might, not by power, but by God's Spirit that I can function. It is in Him that I live and move and have my being. It is He who keeps me from stumbling, He who brings me to the Father, He who works through me. Today I breathe in the breath of God and allow His strength to prove me ABLE.

What a relief to know that it is Christ in me who keeps me from stumbling. It is not my self-discipline, self-actualization, or self-anything that makes me acceptable to God. It is Christ alone. What have you been afraid to step into for fear of failing? Roll that onto Him—He is able!

POSSIBILITIES

Sow your seed in the morning, and at evening let your hands not be idle, for you do not know which will succeed, whether this or that, or whether both will do equally well.

ECCLESIASTES, 11:6, NIV

I name this day POSSIBILITIES. I will explore them all. They are present in the great moments and present in the trials. They are all around me—an endless unfolding.

I open myself to them. Lord, let me be aware when they are presenting so I can step in and give myself to the adventure. Help me to stretch, grow, and develop. Keep me mindful to be prepared because each moment is filled with POSSIBILITIES.

Opportunity meets preparation. God has prepared SO MANY opportunities for you! What are you doing to prepare your heart and mind to explore and seize them? What are you doing to promote growth and develop skills so you can step into the next possibility?

PLOW AND PLANT

Does a farmer plow continually at planting time and never plant a crop? Does he continually break open the clods of the ground and never sow his seed? Once he has leveled its surface, does he not sow dill and cumin, planting his wheat in rows, his barley in its proper place, and his rye in a patch?

ISAIAH 24:24-25, TPT

I name this day PLOW AND PLANT. No farmer ever harvests a crop because he just turned the idea over in his mind.

I will take action today. I will put my hand to the plow and prepare the soil—straight furrows, well turned. I will invest in my future as I faithfully plant seeds that bring the promise of a harvest into tangible reality. Today, I will PLOW AND PLANT!

We were created from the dust of the ground. Our hearts are the soil which must be broken up, turned over, and plowed. Once made ready, we must plant seeds for a faithful harvest. What crop do you desire? What ideas need to be broken and turned over? What seeds of faith and good works need to be planted?

JUNE

After this I looked, and behold, right in front of me
I saw a vast multitude of people—an enormous multitude
so huge that no one could count—made up of victorious
ones from every nation, tribe, people group, and language.
They were all in glistening white robes,
standing before the throne and before the
Lamb with palm branches in their hands.

REVELATION 7:9, TPT

FLOURISH

The righteous will flourish like a palm tree.

PSALM 92:12, NIV

I name this day FLOURISH. I will prosper and thrive. I am like a cedar of Lebanon and I flourish like a palm tree—a myriad of roots to keep me stable, and flexible enough to bend in storms, not break. I am a well-watered vine and all my leaves are green.

I decree vitality, health, and strength in my body today. I decree wisdom and understanding over my mind. I will carefully connect today so my relationships bear much fruit. I am fully alive and I will FLOURISH!

In what areas do you need to develop more flexibility? How is your root system? Are you well-watered? Now that you have answered these questions, draw closer to the Almighty Gardener. It is His desire that you prosper and flourish.

COMMUNITY

*This is how we know what love is: Jesus laid
down His life for us. And we ought to lay down
our lives for our brothers and sisters.*

1 JOHN 3:16, NIV

I name this day COMMUNITY—the real kind that isn't merely polite or social. I desire community that gives and receives life. Makes a difference. Helps. Heals. Celebrates. Strengthens.

I will be the kind of friend I wish to have. I will open my heart to the risks that come from connecting deeply in order to have the chance of the reward that comes from meaningful connection. Today I give myself to participating in meaningful COMMUNITY.

Who is in your circle? With whom do you do life? Are they uplifting, encouraging, and supporting you, or do you find them bringing you down? Today, be intentional about the community with which you surround yourself.

ASK AGAIN

If you then, though you are evil, know how to give good
gifts to your children, how much more will your Father
in heaven give the Holy Spirit to those who ask Him!

LUKE 11:13, NIV

I name this day ASK AGAIN. I desire a fresh outpouring, renewed indwelling, a fathomless filling. Expand my heart, Lord. Enlarge the place of my spirit that I may make room to receive more of Yours. This day, I ASK AGAIN.

What space have you given the Spirit to move within you? Do you find yourself trying to compartmentalize your faith—keep it manageable? Today, come to the Holy Spirit and ask again for a fresh outpouring. Though you may have asked before, ask again and await His response!

IMITATE

Watch what God does, and then you do it, like children who learn proper behavior from their parents. Mostly what God does is love you. Keep company with Him and learn a life of love. Observe how Christ loved us. His love was not cautious but extravagant. He didn't love in order to get something from us but to give everything of Himself to us. Love like that.

EPHESIANS 5:1-2, MSG

I name this day IMITATE. Children learn from imitating adults. Interns learn from imitating professionals. When I encounter someone who has victory or success in an area where I desire to grow, I will observe them so I can imitate what they do. I want to learn what they know and put it into practice.

Today, I'll think about who has good things going on. I will purpose in my heart to IMITATE them!

Think about who you would love to have as a mentor. If practical, reach out and connect with them. If not, find out what they have written or posted as videos and learn what they know. Begin to imitate these practices until they become your own.

SHARED

*Two are better than one, because they have a good
reward for their toil. For if they fall, one will lift
up his fellow. But woe to him who is alone when
he falls and has not another to lift him up!*

ECCLESIASTES 4:9-10, ESV

I name this day SHARED. Living in community with others is better than living alone. Today I am grateful for those in my life and will connect meaningfully with intention.

It's okay to ask for help. It is wise to be accountable to others. The camaraderie and friendships I desire are only possible when life is SHARED.

Life was meant to be lived together, not as a solo act! Though at times it may feel easier to go it alone—especially when feeling guilty or ashamed or unworthy. Remember this: many hands make for light work! There is safety in a multitude of counselors. Who can you share life with today?

FOLLOW

*Then He called the crowd to Him along with His disciples
and said: "Whoever wants to be My disciple must deny
themselves and take up their cross and follow Me."*

MARK 8:34, NIV

I name this day FOLLOW. I have learned that believing saves me, but following sets me free! No turning back. No wavering. I am His disciple.

I will eat what He feeds and I will go where He leads. It is a privilege and a comfort to know that my steps have been ordered by God. I am delighted to FOLLOW.

Believing that a street sign is real is completely different than following its direction! The same is true for Christ: believing in Him is much different than following His footsteps. How can you turn your belief in Him as God into the practical reality of following where He leads?

OPPORTUNITY TO TRUST

We all experience times of testing, which is normal for every
human being. But God will be faithful to you.
He will screen and filter the severity, nature, and timing of
every test or trial you face so that you can bear it.
And each test is an opportunity to trust Him more,
for along with every trial God has provided for you a
way of escape that will bring you out of it victoriously.

1 CORINTHIANS 10:13, TPT

I name this day OPPORTUNITY TO TRUST. Times of testing are normal. They are Father-filtered—the nature, timing, and severity of the testing are all measured by Him and mixed with His grace.

There is a way of escape—a path through each trial that leads me to victory. Even in this hard thing, God, You are faithful. I will reframe this situation and see it as an OPPORTUNITY TO TRUST.

Even when the end of the tunnel bears no light, even when the storm hasn't yet run out of rain, even while you wait for your miracle, you can trust that the same God who brought you to it will bring you through it! Your victory is coming. Oh for grace to trust Him more ...

WISDOM

Wisdom is supreme—so get wisdom.
And whatever else you get, get understanding.

PROVERBS 4:7, CSB

I name this day WISDOM. God says when I ask for it, He will give it. The whole world sought audience with Solomon to hear the wisdom God had placed in his heart. Like Solomon, I desire wisdom.

I am a deep well. The wisdom of God flows through me. I will speak His words and demonstrate His ways. I desire understanding be added to wisdom; that I may develop the ability to skillfully apply the knowledge I have gained. Today, I will walk in WISDOM.

What does it mean to you to have wisdom? Moreover, what do you most need wisdom for in this season? Spend time with God on this today. Ask Him for wisdom. Seek wisdom. God will grant it.

FUTURE HOPE

Know that wisdom is such to your soul; if you find it,
there will be a future, and your hope will not be cut off.

PROVERBS 24:14, ESV

I name this day FUTURE HOPE. Wisdom is like honey, and if I find wisdom, then God promises me a future hope that will not be cut off. Therefore, wisdom is a path to hope!

I decree hope in my heart today. I release hope into the atmosphere. It is like disinfectant, like an antibiotic, like a candle's flame in a dark tunnel. It is an anchor for my soul. Whatever may come, whatever I face, I hold fast to Jesus and firmly embrace my FUTURE HOPE.

Through God's divinely-planted wisdom, you gain access to never-ending hope—hope that will see you through every season that life has to offer. What are you hoping for today? In what area do you need wisdom in order to gain access to future hope?

POSTERITY

Even when I am old and gray, do not forsake me,
my God, till I declare Your power to the next generation,
your mighty acts to all who are to come.

PSALM 71:18, NIV

I name this day POSTERITY. I contend for a generation yet to be born. I invest in the next generation to stir their faith, champion their gifts, and steward their anointing.

I look past my today. I look beyond my tomorrow. My decisions and actions will impact many generations to come. So, I honor the past—embracing all that was good and wise, and I redeem all that was broken or lost. I break generational curses and claim generational blessings given by God. My passion is ignited to lay the foundations for all my POSTERITY.

POSTERITY: all future descendants of a person; the
offspring of one progenitor to the furthest generation.

The next generation will look to you. They will learn from you—the good and the bad. Your character is the scaffolding they will scale to build their lives. Whether in the natural or the spiritual, how can you prepare the way for them?

FOUNTAIN

For with You is the fountain of life;
in Your light do we see light.

PSALM 36:9, ESV

I name this day FOUNTAIN. God is the fountain of life, and I am His. I therefore command, "Spring up, oh well, within my soul!"

I decree the living waters in my belly to rise up and break forth with joy. My soul sings, my heart cries out. I am a pleasing, refreshing FOUNTAIN.

The imagery and symbolism of water is rich within the Bible. Let the Word of God water you. Let the rivers of living water flow from you. Even if you feel dry, by faith step into the wonderful refreshing waters of life. Let the fountain of God fill you until it spills from you.

WONDER AND AWE

How great you are, O Sovereign LORD!
There is no one like You. We have never
even heard of another God like you!

2 SAMUEL 7:22, NLT

I name this day WONDER AND AWE. To be loved by God is a mystery beyond comprehension. That I am in His notice at all, that He is mindful of me astonishes me. His sovereignty is a comfort, His greatness is incomprehensible.

I notice birdsong. I am mindful of the sky's massive expanse, the delicate framework of trees, the incredible symmetry of planets and stars. When I pause to consider the works of Your hands, I cannot help but be filled with WONDER AND AWE.

The same God who numbered the stars has also numbered the hairs on your head! How beautiful it is that God created you with intention, reverence, and purpose. Allow yourself to approach Him as a child today, seeing things for the first time, filled with wonder and awe.

I BELIEVE

Who is it that overcomes the world?
Only the one who believes that Jesus is the Son of God.

1 JOHN 5:5, NIV

I name this day I BELIEVE. I believe in God the Father, Almighty Maker of heaven and earth; in Jesus Christ His only begotten Son, our Lord. I believe in the Holy Spirit, who proceeds from the Father and the Son and is worshipped and glorified. In these three, the beautiful Triune mystery, I BELIEVE.

Is your faith shaken by doubt or fear. In order to overcome, you must first submit yourself to the Overcomer of All—Jesus Christ. His power is free to all who believe. Align your belief with His power. Stretch yourself towards the incomprehensible mysteries and see how miraculous His response to you can be!

AWARENESS

Search me, O God, and know my heart:
try me, and know my thoughts:
And see if there be any wicked way in me,
and lead me in the way everlasting.

PSALM 139:23-24, KJV

I name this day AWARENESS. I am committed to regularly assessing and examining my life. Increased awareness allows me greater opportunity to fulfill my potential. When I dare to explore my shadow projections, the container of my being becomes larger. "Search me and try me," is a bold prayer risking self-exposure.

Today I pray, "Search me and try me, O Lord, see if there be any wicked way in me." I desire my character to grow and become more like Yours. I turn the lights on my thoughts, my words, my attitudes, and my behavior. To become more like You, requires a higher level of AWARENESS.

"The life which is unexamined is not worth living."

— SOCRATES

Take a moment to assess things today—list your goals, priorities, and dreams. Then, assess yourself—your attitudes, your responses, your choices. Are you steering yourself in the direction of your goals, priorities, and dreams? If not, how can you redirect yourself?

PASSION

My heart burned like a fire flaring up within me ...

PSALM 39:3, GW

I name this day PASSION. May the flame in my heart burn so bright and hot it ignites a spark in the hearts of others.

Passion is the fuel that causes me to run hard after my calling, to relentlessly pursue all God has for me and all He desires from me. I surrender it all and let it rise in me unbridled and unbruised. Though the daily grind threatens to put out the flames, today I kindle the fire that beats in my chest. Today, I celebrate PASSION.

What fuels your fire? In other words, what are you passionate about? If your passion has grown pale, take the time to identify it once again. Feed it. Stoke the fires. God honors the pursuit. Run in the direction of your calling!

CROWNED

So, my very dear friends, don't get thrown off course.
Every desirable and beneficial gift comes out of heaven.
The gifts are rivers of light cascading down from the Father
of Light. There is nothing deceitful in God, nothing two-
faced, nothing fickle. He brought us to life using the true
Word, showing us off as the crown of all His creatures.

JAMES 1:17-18, MSG

I name this day CROWNED. When things pile up before me, let me not be thrown off course or become overwhelmed by worry or care. Instead, may I be stunned by the gifts that come from heaven. God, astonish me with Your goodness. Overwhelm me with how You love me and always seem to make a way. Show me Your wonders!

Bring me to life with Your Word. Remind me that I was the one You chose to be CROWNED out of all Your creatures on earth!

When was the last time you truly felt overwhelmed by God's goodness? God reveals Himself to you through the gifts He bestows. You are the crown of all His creatures, and He loves showing you off. How can you delight in this today?

HONOR

*Now unto the King eternal, immortal, invisible, the only
wise God, be honor and glory forever and ever. Amen.*

1 TIMOTHY 1:17, KJV

I name this day HONOR. To the King of Ages, Immortal, Invisible, the only God, be honor and glory forever. Amen.

May my thoughts, words, and deeds represent my desire to nurture a culture of honor in my home and family as well as where I work and live. I will hold others in high esteem, both recognizing and expressing their value. I can make a difference. I can shift atmospheres. I can demolish arguments and tear down walls as I choose to operate in HONOR.

Immortal, Invisible God only wise;
In light inaccessible hid from our eyes.
Most blessed, most glorious, the Ancient of Days;
Almighty, victorious, Thy great name be praised.

—*Hymn by Walter Chalmers Smith*

Today's culture leans away from honor. It calls out and cancels. It bullies and throws ugly words from the safety of social media, avoiding face-to-face communication. It can feel impossible to operate in honor, but it's not. Be counter-cultural. How can you walk in honor?

SIGNIFICANT

*... pray that our God will make you a fit for
what He's called you to be, pray that He'll fill
your good ideas and acts of faith with His own
energy so that it all amounts to something.*

2 THESSALONIANS 1:11, MSG

I name this day SIGNIFICANT. May God make me fit for what He has called me. May He fill my ideas and faith-filled actions with His energy so they amount to something worthwhile. Help me remember that neither the fame nor the blame is on me. I can risk obedience to God because the glory is His.

The results are Yours to measure, God. The obedience is mine to give. Let me remember to walk worthy and trust that as I follow You, it is You—not my efforts—that make my life SIGNIFICANT.

Your work will not go unnoticed by God, even if it does go unnoticed by man. It isn't the size of your following that measures your impact; it is the size of your sacrifice to follow God. If you are struggling or striving to feel significant, surrender your work to Him. Let His energy fill you with fresh joy.

GOD IS A REWARDER

*And it is impossible to please God without faith.
Anyone who wants to come to Him must believe that God
exists and that He rewards those who sincerely seek Him.*

HEBREWS 11:6, NLT

I name this day GOD IS A REWARDER. I sometimes view Him more as a punisher of mistakes, and imagine His great disapproval of my bad habits and dumb choices. But He is actually a rewarder of those who seek Him—mistakes, failed attempts, and all.

Today I choose to simply believe that God exists. I hand Him my flawed and feeble faith. As I seek Him, I relax into the truth that His nature is not to be punitive, rather, GOD IS A REWARDER.

God delights in His children and gives them good gifts. Our faith pleases Him, no matter how great or small. Have you been waiting for the other shoe to drop? For something bad to happen? Ask God to flip your paradigm today. Ask Him to reveal Himself to you as a rewarder—not a punisher.

BRIDGE

And He changes the times and the seasons;
He removes kings and raises up kings;
He gives wisdom to the wise
and knowledge to those who have understanding.

DANIEL 2:21, NKJV

I name this day BRIDGE. As I sense one season is ending, I trust God to provide the bridge of transition that will allow me to cross over to the next.

I may not see clearly what is up ahead, but I know this "expansion bridge" will bring me to the place He has appointed for me to grow. I decree my faith to rise so I may step out into the unknown, trusting His heart for me and knowing that over any troubled waters I must cross, He is my BRIDGE.

The start of a new season can feel daunting. No one loves the unknown, but you can rest in this truth: greater things have yet to come! What uncertainties challenge your heart as you begin to move towards your next season? Hand these to God today.

PURSUIT

Wise men and women are always learning,
always listening for fresh insights.

PROVERBS 18:15, MSG

I name this day PURSUIT. I am always learning, always listening for fresh insights.

I desire wisdom, increased understanding, higher awareness, and greater compassion. To that end, I intentionally go after God's Word and God's ways. These are my passionate PURSUIT.

What are you listening to? What are you reading? In what ways are you allowing yourself to be challenged? Take a moment today to become more intentional in your pursuit.

ON TRACK

He stooped down to lift me out of danger
from the desolate pit I was in,
out of the muddy mess I had fallen into.
Now He's lifted me up into a firm, secure place
and steadied me while I walk along His ascending path.

PSALM 40:2, TPT

I name this day ON TRACK. I swerve neither right nor left. I stay my course—straight ahead. I am firm and secure.

I decree solid rails before me. I know God has prepared the path toward my next destination. My decisions become more steady when I have a clear path and I know that I am ON TRACK.

Sometimes it is good to remember where you came from, what God has brought you out of. There is grace in gratitude. When you feel unsteady or unsure, remember that God walks beside you. It is He who steadies your steps and keeps you on the path of righteousness.

ENERGETIC

Indolence wants it all and gets nothing;
the energetic have something to show for their lives.

PROVERBS 13:4, MSG

I name this day ENERGETIC. I will apply purposeful activity to my plans and dreams.

Wishing wants it all, but without action it gets nothing. Seeds of faith must be planted. Faith without works is dead. I want something to show for my life. Therefore, I put action to my dreams. I am ENERGETIC.

What have you been putting off? What needs your attention, but has been too inconvenient to invest time and energy into developing? Today is a good day to shake off excuses and initiate action.

CATCH THE WIND

So don't be so surprised when I tell you that you have to be "born from above"—out of this world, so to speak. You know well enough how the wind blows this way and that. You hear it rustling through the trees, but you have no idea where it comes from or where it's headed next. That's the way it is with everyone "born from above" by the wind of God, the Spirit of God.

JOHN 3:8, MSG

I name this day CATCH THE WIND. No matter which way the wind blows or where it comes from, I will trim my sails to catch it and keep my momentum, to stay on course.

I decree smooth sailing today. I am born from above. I declare the wind of the Spirit to blow over me, to surround me and propel me forward. I move ahead with joy as I ride the wave and CATCH THE WIND.

Have you ever felt like things are stacked against you? Like you are constantly trying to move against the current? When this happens, instead of dropping anchor and waiting for more favorable conditions, what can you do to trim the sails and use the adversity and resistance to push you forward?

DRAW IT UP

*Then God opened (Hagar's) eyes, and she saw
a well of water. And she went and filled the
skin with water and gave the boy a drink.*

GENESIS 21:19, ESV

I name this day DRAW IT UP. I will draw living water from the deep wells that have been faithfully dug, I will draw up what I need to flourish in this season.

I will plunge my bucket into that hidden, underground source of refreshing, and by faith, it will be filled to overflowing, submerged in goodness and revelation. No matter the drought on the surface, I have a well from which I may faithfully DRAW IT UP.

Even when you feel like your resources are depleted, when you do not know what to do or how to proceed, God has the resources already prepared for you. What do you need today? Ask God to point you to the well from which you can draw.

MERITORIOUS

*I tell you this timeless truth:
The person who follows Me in faith,
believing in Me, will do the same mighty
miracles that I do—even greater miracles than
these because I go to be with My Father!*

JOHN 14:12, TPT

I name this day MERITORIOUS. Great miracles are possible today! May today be praiseworthy, laudable, and excellent in every way.

I decree the favor of God goes before me. I will rise to His potential placed in me. I will do exploits because I follow Him in faith. His power is working through me. Because of His grace, this day is MERITORIOUS!

*MERITORIOUS: deserving reward
or praise, praiseworthy.*

Every day we have the invitation to step out of the ordinary and into the supernatural. Miracles are not reserved for super special occasions. Because your are His and you walk in faith, believing in Him, miracles are part of His plan for you. What miracle will you believe for today?

ENDURANCE

By your endurance you will gain your lives.

LUKE 21:19, ESV

I name this day ENDURANCE. I will walk with a calm spirit and allow time for things to unfold without pushing them to my timetable.

I decree steadfastness. I declare peace to surround my heart and soothe my mind. I will see the end from the beginning and appreciate the process of development required to get there. I won't give up. God, grant me ENDURANCE.

Endurance is not easy. Process is not easy. Waiting on God's timing is one of the hardest things to do. Don't give up. Ask God to renew your strength today and give you confirmation that He has a plan for your harvest. Stay the course!

JUNE 28

PERSPECTIVE

*Since you have been raised to new life with Christ,
set your sights on the realities of heaven,
where Christ sits in the place of honor at God's right hand.
Think about the things of heaven, not the things of earth.*

COLOSSIANS 3:1-2, NLT

I name this day PERSPECTIVE. I will do my best to try out a new one—a heavenly one.

I embrace the strategy of a clear vantage point. I process the present through a new lens and decree clarity of vision. I soar with the Spirit, high above the problem. As I gain that bird's eye view, I will trust wisdom's PERSPECTIVE.

Perspective is a gift. Perspective provides context, and that context can help you understand what you are going through right now. Ask God to open your eyes today, to grant you a new perspective. Ask Him to let you see with the eyes of the Spirit.

DETERMINATION

If your faith remains strong, even while surrounded by life's difficulties, you will continue to experience the untold blessings of God! True happiness comes as you pass the test with faith, and receive the victorious crown of life promised to every lover of God!

JAMES 1:12, TPT

I name this day DETERMINATION. A glimpse of purpose wrapped in promise is worth enduring a process.

I declare strength into my weariness today. I decree help to manifest through unexpected sources. My faith will remain strong. I command energy in my spirit, clarity in my mind, and joy in my soul. I am filled with DETERMINATION.

God's blessings are rich, even in times of trial or testing. Ask God to show you His purpose. Remind yourself of His promises over you so you can embrace the process with the determination of joy.

RADIATE WITH HOPE

*Now may God, the fountain of hope, fill you to
overflowing with uncontainable joy and perfect
peace as you trust in Him. And may the power of
the Holy Spirit continually surround your life with His
super-abundance until you radiate with hope!*

ROMANS 15:13, TPT

I name this day RADIATE WITH HOPE. Because I place my trust in God and do not allow circumstances to dictate my confidence, I have hope.

I decree the substance of things I hope for to manifest, and the evidence of things I do not yet see to become clear. My soul's anchor holds me steadfastly, even in stormy seas I trust in Him. His power surrounds my life. I RADIATE WITH HOPE.

Are you in need of hope today? Could you use some uncontainable joy and perfect peace? Trust Him. Give Him the things which concern you and ask His fountain of hope to fill you.

JULY

For the Lord is the Spirit, and wherever the
Spirit of the Lord is, there is freedom.

2 CORINTHIANS 3:17, NLT

FOR THE JOY

For the joy that lay before Him,
He endured the cross.

HEBREWS 12:2, CSB

I name this day FOR THE JOY. My life poured out grows glory. It isn't for my gain or advantage that I sacrifice, but to serve and build others. When I am tired, when I am weary, when self cries to be pampered or petted, I remember the example of my Savior. I think of what Christ endured because of the joy that was set before Him, and my resolve to endure is renewed.

Today, I remember my why—my reason for laying down my life. It is FOR THE JOY that lies before me.

Past wounds take their toll. We become masters of self-protection to guard against future pain? But the walls behind which we retreat, also keep us from pouring our lives out. Don't allow your past to keep you from the joy that lies ahead. Who is your why? Who is your joy?

ENLIGHTENED

*And [I pray] that the eyes of your heart [the very center
and core of your being] may be enlightened [flooded
with light by the Holy Spirit], so that you will know and
cherish the hope [the divine guarantee, the confident
expectation] to which He has called you, the riches of
His glorious inheritance in the saints (God's people) ...*

EPHESIANS 1:18, AMP

I name this day ENLIGHTENED. God, open my eyes and help me
see—in the natural and in the spiritual. Show me Your glory in
everyday objects—in birds and trees and flowers. Reveal Yourself
in the smile of a child, in a work of art, and the pages of a book.
Flood me with the Holy Spirit's light and show me spiritual riches.
Quicken me to the expectation of my calling. With hope and great
gratitude I humbly ask to be ENLIGHTENED.

---

*In the mysteries, in the complexities of life, in the dark and unknown,
God can restore your spiritual vision. You will see His wonders! What do
you need Him to open your eyes to today?*

AT CALVARY

"He Himself bore our sins" in His body on the cross,
so that we might die to sins and live for righteousness ..."

1 PETER 2:24a, NIV

I name this day AT CALVARY. I was reminded this morning of the words of the hymn:

> Years, I spent in vanity and pride,
> Caring not my Lord was crucified,
> Knowing not it was for me He died
> On Calvary

> Mercy there was great and grace was free;
> Pardon there was multiplied to me;
> There my burdened soul found liberty,
> AT CALVARY!

The sacrifice of Jesus birthed new mercy, new grace, and new, unbridled joy! This act of love restored our fallen heart to the Father. Pause today. Consider and celebrate what took place at Calvary—you are a new and pure creation!

DANGEROUS FREEDOM

For freedom Christ has set us free; stand firm therefore,
and do not submit again to a yoke of slavery.

GALATIANS 5:1, ESV

I name this day DANGEROUS FREEDOM. I understand all freedom comes with a price. I know that freedom requires responsibility to stay free.

But freedom is such a joyous, marvelous, beautiful thing it is worth fighting for. Today I combat every thought that would hold my mind captive or seek to displace my identity. My freedom will not allow me to become sin's slave or iniquity to be my master. Instead, I am free to walk in love, power, and a sound mind. I walk in DANGEROUS FREEDOM!

> *"I prefer dangerous freedom over peaceful slavery."*
>
> —*Thomas Jefferson, 1787*

What is an area where you feel bound? What holds your thoughts captive and squeezes joy and life from your heart? Step into Christ's freedom today. Ask God to restore you as His child—free!

BREATH OF FRESH AIR

*Do everything readily and cheerfully—no bickering,
no second-guessing allowed! Go out into the
world uncorrupted, a breath of fresh air in this
squalid and polluted society. Provide people with
a glimpse of good living and of the living God.*

PHILIPPIANS 2:14-15, MSG

I name this day BREATH OF FRESH AIR. I carry the wind of the Spirit, a light breeze of kindness, a gentle reminder of the purity of heaven. May my life provide a glimpse of the living God and to the cynical or disillusioned soul, let me be a BREATH OF FRESH AIR.

What seems to be squeezing the air right out of you? In what area does it feel impossible to catch your breath? The Holy Spirit has breathed a breath of fresh air right back into your tired, strained lungs. Pause and breathe in deeply and slowly. Let this natural act take on a spiritual reality.

IT COUNTS

Abram believed the LORD,
and He credited it to him as righteousness.

GENESIS 15:6, CSB

I name this day IT COUNTS. Sometimes just to believe—in the face of contradictions, in the absence of change—requires much faith. Believing is holy. To believe is miraculous.

Your belief—your faith—pleases God and He sees it as righteousness. God is paying attention, and when it takes all you've got to continue standing on what you believe about God, believe me; IT COUNTS.

What makes it challenging for you to keep the faith in this season? What things are making your steps feel labored? Whether it feels like a baby step or a giant leap of faith, when you stand firm and hold onto your belief—it counts!

OVERCOME

And they overcame and conquered him because
of the BLOOD OF THE LAMB and because of
the WORD OF THEIR TESTIMONY ...

REVELATION 12:11, AMP

I name this day OVERCOME. I honor my story—all of it, surrendering it to God, applying the blood of the Lamb to every detail. In this way, I emerge the victor, completely conquering my soul's enemy.

> The blood of the Lamb
>
> + The word of my testimony (my story)
>
> = I OVERCOME

When the war wages on, you will overcome as you apply the blood of the Lamb to your story! Have you given your story thought? When was the last time you shared your testimony? Open yourself to opportunities to share what God has brought you through with someone else. Watch how you begin to overcome.

PEACE THAT TRANSCENDS

Don't be pulled in different directions or worried about a thing. Be saturated in prayer throughout each day, offering your faith-filled requests before God with overflowing gratitude. Tell Him every detail of your life, then God's wonderful peace that transcends human understanding, will guard your heart and mind through Jesus Christ.

PHILIPPIANS 4:6-7, TPT

I name this day PEACE THAT TRANSCENDS. Because I cast my cares on Him, I am anxious for nothing. It is not because I have the absence of conflict, but because I am in the presence of Someone that I experience the supernatural reality of PEACE THAT TRANSCENDS.

Are you anxious? Do you feel the weight of what has yet to pass? Through Christ, you have access to peace that goes beyond your understanding. It is more than enough to get you through. Whatever your lot may be, it is well. It is well. Let the peace of Christ dwell in you richly today.

SEE THE GLORY

Jesus said to her, "Didn't I tell you that if you believed,
you would see the glory of God?"

JOHN 11:40, CSB

I name this day SEE THE GLORY. I believe.

My heart has settled on the goodness of God. I trust His sovereignty, even in the midst of sacred struggle. His arm is not short, He never fails, and I am fully persuaded that I will SEE THE GLORY of God!

Do you find it harder to trust in times of struggle? Cast your cares on the Lord—roll them over onto Him. You will only see God's glory when looking through the lens of your belief!

PATIENT IN HOPE

*The Lord is not slow in keeping His promise,
as some understand slowness. Instead He is
patient with you, not wanting anyone to perish,
but everyone to come to know repentance.*

2 PETER 3:9, NIV

I name this day PATIENT IN HOPE. God plays the long game with us, holding out for a lasting, eternal reward. He is not in a hurry; He has eternity in mind.

Today I surrender to His timing with those I love. With them (and myself) I shall stand and remain PATIENT IN HOPE.

Time is a paradox—one moment can feel like a lifetime, but a lifetime also passes in a single moment. Are you counting down the days or are you making the days count? Trust Him with the thing that seems to be taking too long to resolve. Be patient in hope—if God is in no hurry, why should you be?

BE STILL

He says, "Be still and know that I am God;
I will be exalted among the nations,
I will be exalted in the earth."

PSALM 46:10, NIV

I name this day BE STILL. I rebuke the wind and waves. I will allow no storm to deter me from my destiny. My God is with me and His peace surpasses my understanding. It guards my heart and mind.

I decree safety today: over my spirit, over my soul, and over my body. Whatever encircles me, whatever tries to make troubled waters, it is no match for God at work in me. I command the storm inside my mind to be quiet. "Peace, BE STILL."

What storms are circling your mind? Do you find it difficult to catch a breath in the midst of them? Know this: if God brought you to it, He will bring you through it. Be still. Be still and know that He is God. As God, He has His hand on you in this storm.

FUTURE HARVEST

Then He said to His disciples,
"The harvest is [indeed] plentiful,
but the workers are few.
So pray to the Lord of the harvest
to send out workers into His harvest.

MATTHEW 9:37-38, AMP

I name this day FUTURE HARVEST. I will plant intentional seeds and carefully nurture what I desire to grow. I will prune what is now unruly and be faithful to uproot what bears bad fruit.

I declare fertile soil in my life. I decree conditions favorable for seeds to take root and grow strong and sure. I will look for opportunities today to plant, weed, water, and tend to my FUTURE HARVEST.

What crops do you want to harvest within your soul? List a few. Have you begun planting those seeds? More importantly, is the soil of your heart fostering life and growth? Your present actions will influence your future harvest—choose wisely!

STRONG

*Be strong in the Lord
and in His mighty power.*

EPHESIANS 6:10, NIV

I name this day STRONG. I am strong in the Lord and His mighty power.

I decree strength into my body—freedom from fatigue, freedom from aches and pains. I release vitality to flow through my veins. I declare my mind is being renewed, my character is being strengthened, and that every part of me—spirit, soul, and body, mind, will, and emotions—is STRONG.

*STRONG: able to withstand great force or
pressure, well fortified, unassailable.*

Because of God's mighty power, you are strong! Where do you feel the weakest? How can you shift your focus from your weakness to His strength today? Rise up, mighty warrior, and step into strength. Decree it over yourself and activate the power of God over your life.

204

FAINT NOT

So we do not lose heart.
Though our outer self is wasting away,
our inner self is being renewed day by day.

2 CORINTHIANS 4:16, ESV

I name this day FAINT NOT. My light and momentary troubles are achieving a weight of glory that far outweighs them all.

I decree a "faint not" spirit arise within me as I am being renewed day by day. I will reap in due season. I declare strength into my body and into my mind. I speak to my spirit and command that it FAINT NOT.

What race are you running? Whether it be a 400 meter dash or a marathon, do not lose heart! Allow Him to renew you, day by day. The race you run may be long, but through Him you will endure!

LIMITLESS

Do you have any idea how powerful God is?
Have you ever heard of a teacher like Him?
Has anyone ever had to tell Him what to do,
or correct Him, saying, "You did that all wrong!"?

JOB 36:22-23, MSG

I name this day LIMITLESS! The sky is not the limit, only the borders of my mind can keep me from the limitless potential I have in God.

I decree the blinders off. I declare dreams to expand, vision to increase, and creativity to soar. I will not doubt His power. I am energized, and I release my imagination to approach the reality that God is LIMITLESS!

What is the biggest dream you have? Allow yourself to reach deep and unbury it. Did you know that even your wildest dreams are within reach through God? Dream big today—In Him, you are limitless!

ECHO LOVE

*Above all, constantly echo God's intense love
for one another, for love will be a
canopy over a multitude of sins.*

1 PETER 4:8, TPT

I name this day ECHO LOVE. To do this, I must be close enough to God for His released love to bounce off me and reflect back to Him. I want to vibrate with love's frequency, and in that wave carry mercy and grace, charity and compassion. I cover, hem in, and canopy others when I ECHO LOVE.

How closely are you walking with God? In your day-to-day life, do you get close enough to resonate with the frequency of heaven, to echo His love? As you go about your day, take moments to draw nearer so that you can echo the love of God.

TOTAL TRUST

But blessed is the one who trusts in the
LORD, whose confidence is in Him.

JEREMIAH 17:7, NIV

I name this day TOTAL TRUST. I will trust when I clearly see and understand, or when the way is foggy and I have no clue. When it all lines up and makes sense, and when it all falls apart and I am troubled, I will trust. On top, on bottom, or in the middle of a curve, the One I love is a steady, present help.

God's plans for me are good, and the scope of their unfolding is eternal—there is time for all things to yet work for my good. In You, God, I place my TOTAL TRUST.

God's way is always better, higher, stronger, and clearer than mine. It's hard to completely surrender control, but the payoff is endless. He has promised to work things out for your good. What do you need to place into His capable hands today? What part of your heart is struggling to yield total trust to God?

RESPONSIBLE

It's true that our freedom allows us to do anything,
but that doesn't mean that everything we do
is good for us. I'm free to do as I choose, but I
choose to never be enslaved to anything.

1 CORINTHIANS 6:12, TPT

I name this day RESPONSIBLE. The purpose of liberty is not to live without any constraints. It is the freedom to choose how to live.

Today I will look at my temporal future through the lens of eternity, and I will make wise decisions and good choices that serve my larger goals. I will honor God by exercising wisdom and doing that which is RESPONSIBLE.

Paul said, "All things are lawful for me, but not all things are helpful."
My dad used to tell me, "Others can, but you can't." Grace is not a
license to live senselessly. Weigh your choices on the scale of wisdom,
and let mature responsibility win the day.

UNEXPECTED

Surprise us with love at daybreak;
then we'll skip and dance all the day long.

PSALM 90:14, MSG

I name this day UNEXPECTED. Those who have made promises and let me down … I won't worry about them. God is going to show up in the unlikely places, through people who owe me nothing and haven't promised me one thing!

Spirit, get ready for the unexpected. Prepare to be surprised and amazed. Instead of setting myself up for another disappointment, I will prepare for the unlikely. I open myself up for the (perhaps unremarkable in the moment) divine appointment. Today, I give myself over to experience the UNEXPECTED!

How do you feel about surprises? Are you more of a "go-with-the-flow" person, or does uncertainty make you uneasy? God works for your good, even when you can't see or understand it. Today, reach for the unexpected. Open yourself up to be surprised by His goodness.

NEW THING

Behold, I will do a new thing.
Now it shall spring forth;
Shall you not know it?
I will even make a road in the wilderness
and rivers in the desert.

ISAIAH 43:19, NKJV

I name this day NEW THING! My mind is open to new possibilities, new patterns of thought, and new ways of looking at things. There's a way in my wilderness and rivers in my desert. I am open, I am seeking, I am engaged. Bring on the NEW THING!

What deserts have you been stuck in? Do you feel lost in the wilderness, left behind? God is doing a new thing in you, child, and He has not left you alone. Allow the new thing to spring forth. It may be but a tender shoot, but it holds the promise of life and growth.

CONNECTIONS

*I am contending for you that your hearts will be
wrapped in the comfort of heaven and woven
together into love's fabric. This will give you access
to all the riches of God as you experience the
revelation of God's great mystery—Christ.*

COLOSSIANS 2:2, TPT

I name this day CONNECTIONS. God brings me divine connections as links in destiny's chain. I will honor every relationship He brings me and be open to engage with divine appointments. God, weave us together.

I give thanks for those to whom I am connected, with whom I share life. Honor is the currency of influence. I will intentionally cultivate honor with each and every one of my divine CONNECTIONS.

Meaningful, intentional connection will draw you (and those you connect with) closer to the Father. Who are you connecting with today? What love and good deeds can you show them?

SERVE IN LOVE

*It is absolutely clear that God has called you to a free
life. Just make sure that you don't use this freedom as an
excuse to do whatever you want to do and destroy your
freedom. Rather, use your freedom to serve one another in
love; that's how freedom grows. For everything we know
about God's Word is summed up in a single sentence: Love
others as you love yourself. That's an act of true freedom.*

GALATIANS 5:13-14, MSG

I name this day SERVE IN LOVE. I will love others in the same way I
love myself. My freedom in Christ is freedom from my old, selfish,
sinful nature. It is freedom to live in my renewed, God-breathed,
God-fashioned identity.

I value this freedom, and I understand the price paid that I might
live free. When I am self-serving, I destroy that freedom. So today,
as an act of true freedom, I will SERVE IN LOVE.

*How can you serve in love today? What is in your power to do that will
demonstrate your love for God and the joy you have because you are
free to live as His child? Make serving in love a priority today.*

JULY 23

FRUIT THAT REMAINS

You have not chosen Me, but I have chosen you and I
have appointed and placed and purposefully planted
you, so that you would go and bear fruit and keep
on bearing, and that your fruit will remain and be
lasting, so that whatever you ask of the Father in My
name [as My representative] He may give to you.

JOHN 15:16, AMP

I name this day FRUIT THAT REMAINS. God, you chose me. You appointed, placed, and purposefully planted me so I could bear lasting fruit. Develop the fruit of the Spirit in me. May love, joy, peace, patience, kindness, goodness, faithfulness, gentleness, and self-control grow and mature as I abide in the Vine.

Teach me, Father, how to live in union with You, rooted and grounded, well-watered and well-seasoned so my life will bear FRUIT THAT REMAINS.

Each season finds us with different levels of fruitfulness. Sometimes our crop is abundant, and some years our fruit is shriveled or full of worms. What does it mean to you to bear lasting fruit? How does your life represent fruit that remains?

EXCEPTIONAL

Do you see a man skillful in his work?
He will stand before kings;
he will not stand before obscure men.

PROVERBS 22:29, ESV

I name this day EXCEPTIONAL. I will press through even when my energy is spent.

I will stay focused on the goal. If it is too large and too far away, I will focus on a smaller, closer goal that takes me in the direction of the bigger goal. I decree excellence over my endeavors and embrace the challenge of becoming EXCEPTIONAL.

Mediocrity is easy. Excuses come naturally. Focus requires determination. Gaining mastery at any skill requires investment. Are you committed to excellence or skating by? What is an area where you have natural gifting that if you applied yourself, you could become exceptional?

SERENITY

You heavens above, rain down my righteousness;
let the clouds shower it down.
Let the earth open wide, let salvation spring up,
let righteousness flourish with it;
I, the Lord, have created it.

ISAIAH 45:8, NIV

I name this day SERENITY. I will drink in calmness like a gentle rain falling in the woods. I will embrace the ability to be untroubled.

I actively lay aside my cares. I bring forward in my mind all the many blessings I enjoy. I listen to the music created by a steady shower, breaking upon the leaves as it makes its fall from the heavens. As rain covers the earth, I am covered in the goodness of God. I let His river of peace fill me with SERENITY.

Rain is a blessing. It replenishes the earth. Floods upon dry ground are a symbol of washing away sin. Whenever rain falls, I am reminded of the goodness of God, the cycles of life, and the passing of seasons. Close your eyes and let your mind hear the rain falling. Be filled with the peace of God's promise.

VITALITY

So you must remain in life-union with Me,
for I remain in life-union with you.
For as a branch severed from the vine will not
bear fruit, so your life will be fruitless unless
you live your life intimately joined to Mine.

JOHN 15:4, TPT

I name this day VITALITY. I abide with Jesus. I remain in life-union with Him, intimately joined.

My life joined to His brings an increase of faith, favor, and anointing. I will intentionally nurture the things I desire to grow. I will be faithful to develop that which He has placed in my heart. Because I abide with Him, I am filled with VITALITY.

VITALITY: the power giving continuance of life,
the capacity to live and develop.

Nothing compares to living in life-union with Jesus, and nothing feels more empty than being disconnected from the Vine. What does it mean to you to abide in Christ? What does intimacy with the Father look like for you? Explore this with Him today.

JULY 27

LIKE A RIVER

*And wherever the river goes, every living creature that
swarms will live, and there will be very many fish.
For this water goes there, that the waters of the sea may
become fresh; so everything will live where the river goes.*

EZEKIEL 47:9, ESV

I name this day LIKE A RIVER. I will flow. I will roll with things. When I encounter an obstacle, I will cut a new path.

I decree grace over my mind. I speak peace over my emotional state. I command the atmosphere around me to experience heaven's filter and reflect the glory of God I carry. My prayer today is that living water will flow forth from me LIKE A RIVER.

*What do you carry? What flows forth from your life—from your mouth?
Are you a river of living water or do you better resemble the Dead Sea?
Ask God today to fill you with fresh waters and release the life He has
into a lost and dry land.*

218

OPEN DOOR

*I know your deeds. See, I have placed before you
an open door that no one can shut.
I know that you have little strength, yet you have
kept My word and have not denied My name.*

REVELATION 3:8, NIV

I name this day OPEN DOOR. There are opportunities in front of me requiring risk, personal sacrifice, and uncertainty.

Today I choose to embrace what You have placed in my path, knowing I might fail; but also aware that I just might succeed. I choose to invest in my growth, to mix action with faith, to stretch beyond my comfort and risk adventure with You. No one can shut what you have opened. I will walk through the OPEN DOOR.

What a comfort to know that the free will of man cannot shut doors that God has opened for you. Not even you can mess up badly enough to close a door prepared by Him. Ask Him to show you the path to the open door that awaits you.

GRACE-FILLED

And from the overflow of His fullness
we received grace heaped upon more grace!

JOHN 1:16, TPT

I name this day GRACE-FILLED. I will extend great grace to everyone in my path, and I will thank God for the grace which has been heaped up upon me.

As life's pressures squeeze, may the crushing produce fragrant oil. Lord, may You find an undivided heart in me. May my praise rise as incense. May Your presence infuse me, overwhelm me and instruct me how to live as one GRACE-FILLED.

Would you describe yourself as grace-filled? Do you respond to others from the overflow of God's fullness, or do you find yourself snipping and scowling, demanding and commanding? Receive His grace today. Step into grace heaped upon more grace and be filled to overflowing!

CHRIST ALONE

Both riches and honor come from You, and You rule over all. In Your hand are power and might, and in Your hand it is to make great and to give strength to all. But who am I, and what is my people, that we should be able thus to offer willingly? For all things come from You, and of Your own have we given You.

1 CHRONICLES 29:12, 14, ESV

I name this day CHRIST ALONE. All that I have comes from You. Anything I give back to You came from You to begin with. Every good and perfect gift has come from Your hand—all power, all might, all honor, all dominion, all strength.

Whenever I feel as though there is anything in which I can boast, help me to remember that my source is CHRIST ALONE.

Pause today and reverently acknowledge the power and greatness of God. Survey your possessions—where did they come from? Survey your skills—from where do they flow? Speak out your gratitude today to the One who has given you everything.

LAVISH

See what great love the Father
has lavished on us,
that we should be called children of God!
And that is what we are!

1 JOHN 3:1a, NIV

I name this day LAVISH. I embrace the extravagance of God's grace, the richness of His love, and the splendor of His majesty.

What great love the Father has lavished upon me! He anoints my head with oil and my cup runneth over. God pours out generously and I position myself to receive His LAVISH goodness.

LAVISH: to bestow something in generous
or extravagant quantities.

It can be hard to imagine what it is like to have someone lavish good things upon you. Extravagant generosity is a rare human experience. Yet God your Father wants to lavish you with His love. Don't be shy today. It isn't spiritual to expect crumbs. Let Him lavish His love upon you!

AUGUST

Why is everyone hungry for more?
"More, more," they say.
"More, more."
I have God's more-than-enough,
more joy in one ordinary day
than they get in all their shopping sprees.
At day's end I'm ready for sound sleep,
For You, God, have put my life back together.

PSALM 4:6-8, MSG

RECOVER

"Are you tired? Worn out? Burned out on religion?
Come to me. Get away with me and you'll recover your life.
I'll show you how to take a real rest.
Walk with me and work with me—watch how I do it.
Learn the unforced rhythms of grace.
I won't lay anything heavy or ill-fitting on you.
Keep company with me and you'll learn
to live freely and lightly."

MATTHEW 11:28-30, MSG

I name this day RECOVER. Teach me how to walk and work with You, God. Teach me how to live freely and lightly. I want to enter the unforced rhythms of grace, to experience the flow of energy and vitality for which I was created.

I want to rise in the morning, refreshed. I want to lay my head down at night, unburdened, knowing my rest will be sweet. Show me how to take a real rest. Teach me how to come away and RECOVER.

When was the last time you truly rested with the Lord? Today, I challenge you to get away with God. Let Him show you how to enter the unforced rhythms of grace. Make time for a nap—if that's not practical today, plan a day where you can unplug, pull away, and recover from life's burdens.

SEE SOMETHING NEW

*Now my eyes will be open and my ears attentive
to the prayer that is made in this place.*

2 CHRONICLES 7:15, ESV

I name this day SEE SOMETHING NEW. Show me something today I have never before seen. Open my eyes to things that have been near me always but remain untouched; things I have never before experienced. Make me attentive in this place, in this moment. Open my eyes that I may SEE SOMETHING NEW.

It's easy to grow accustomed to the world around you—its sights, marvels, and divinely placed opportunities—until they seem commonplace and unremarkable. There are wonders all arround you! Ask God to help you see something new today.

LOVE

*God's love was revealed among us in this way:
God sent His one and only Son into the world
so that we might live through Him.*

1 JOHN 4:9, CSB

I name this day LOVE. I receive the love which has been poured out for me. It has changed me profoundly. That change is best expressed through loving others as I have been loved.

My curiosity is aroused, I want to explore new heights and richer depths of Your love today. Take me beyond my comprehension. Let me experience Your love in new and profound ways. Today in every way, may I be light, may I be salt, may I be LOVE.

In the love of God, your identity lies. It is as simple and as beautiful as this: His blood made you clean. Jesus' sacrifice restored your union with the Triune God. In what ways has this transformative love changed you? How can you express this love to others?

EMPATHY

When someone gets to the end of his rope,
I feel the desperation in my bones.
When someone is duped into sin,
an angry fire burns in my gut.

2 CORINTHIANS 11:29, MSG

I name this day EMPATHY. I do not stand alone in sorrow or in joy. I am connected to others, arm-in-arm, heart-to-heart. I feel what they feel. I join them in life though it cost me my own. Today I shift my awareness beyond myself, and I choose to notice the plight of others. I choose to enter into their grief with them, sit with them in their sorrow, comfort them in their distress.

Because of my great love for you, God, I choose to walk in EMPATHY.

EMPATHY: the ability to sense other
people's emotions; taking on the perspective
of another, able to identify with and
understand their emotions.

When one part of your body is sick or injured, you feel it even in parts of your body that are unafflicted. The same is true for the Church—when one member aches, other members will feel it! How can you link arm-in-arm to share empathy with others?

SHARE THE BURDEN

Share each other's burdens,
and in this way obey the law of Christ.

GALATIANS 6:2, NLT

I name this day SHARE THE BURDEN. As surely as many hands make light work, many souls lighten the heavy heart. I am part of a family—a tribe—and not meant to shoulder things in isolation.

The amazing thing is when I see someone in pain and I reach out or speak out, I access incredible levels of grace. This act—loving God and loving others—allows me to experience the outpouring of heaven's resources. I am never more strong than when I am willing to SHARE THE BURDEN.

Burdens are far too heavy to carry alone—it is important to share the weight of them with others. What burdens are you carrying that you need to share with someone else? In what way can you share someone else's burden?

FRESH MERCY

Great is His faithfulness;
His mercies begin afresh each morning.

LAMENTATIONS 3:23, NLT

I name this day FRESH MERCY. God's love does not run out, it never dries up or wanes. He is faithful even when I am faithless.

God, I step into fresh grace today. Your steadfast love never ceases. Your mercy never comes to an end. Great is Your faithfulness to me! Each morning when I awaken, there You are, still loving me and extending to me FRESH MERCY.

Even when you feel as though you don't deserve mercy, even when you think you are at the end of your rope, God's fresh mercy is available to you. What do you need fresh mercy over today?

WAIT TO SEE

Use all Your skill to put me together;
I wait to see Your finished product.
God, give Your people a break
from this run of bad luck.

PSALM 25:21-22, MSG

I name this day WAIT TO SEE. When in a storm and squall after squall unleashes, it leaves the spirit wet and weary. Things totally unrelated to the struggle become heavy—too heavy, and the light and joy onced lived in seems but a memory. I can pray this prayer for myself or others: "God, when I'm falling apart, put me back together."

I hear You say, "It's not as bad as it seems. My plans for you are good and not evil. I will work this for your good and perfect that which concerns you. This is the process to a finished work."

With hope and trust I can answer, "I WAIT TO SEE."

Though the destination will be beautiful, some of the pit-stops along the way are hard. Every storm, every dark night, every ache and pain— they have all brought you to this moment. The process is a valuable part of your journey. What finished work are you believing for—waiting to see—in this season?

HE KNOWS IT

For the devil's come down on you with both feet;
he's had a great fall; he's wild and raging with
anger; he hasn't much time and he knows it.

REVELATION 12:7-12, MSG

I name this day HE KNOWS IT. The enemy's days for free-for-all are numbered. Though he has unleashed his best attack, my God is greater. Heaven's hosts encamp around me and I join in their chorus of victory and praise. No, the enemy hasn't much time, and HE KNOWS IT!

What battle are you fighting today? Well, it can't go on forever—the enemy has already been defeated! He has been cast as far as the east is from the west by God's might. The enemy's time is short and he knows it! Celebrate your coming victory today!

PEACEMAKER

Those who plan peace have joy.

PROVERBS 12:20, ESV

I name this day PEACEMAKER. I will seek peace and pursue it. I will cast all my anxieties on Him, because He cares for me. Because I trust Him and because my mind is stayed upon Him, He will keep me in perfect peace.

I decree that from the place of peace, I am a peacemaker. As much as depends on me, I will be at peace with all men. I will not shrink from conflict nor will I keep silent in the presence of adversity. I understand that sometimes peace requires war. Only in the absence of conflict with the objective Word of God will I find the courage and ability to walk as a PEACEMAKER.

Walk in peace's direction—it won't always be smooth waters, but you will always be able to adjust your sails. Being a peacemaker requires living from a place of peace in your heart. Even though you can pray for peace, you must also actively pursue it. How can you pursue peace today?

AUGUST 10

REMAIN

*If you remain in Me
and My words remain in you,
ask whatever you wish,
and it will be done for you.*

JOHN 15:7, NIV

I name this day REMAIN. May I step into the steady grace required to stay centered in God and be filled with His Word continuously. Positionally, I am in Christ—His righteousness is mine because I am His.

Intentionally, by faith and practice, I am also in the Lord—my actions, attitudes, and motives are righteouse because of my choice to abide in the Vine. God, I don't want to ask for things that are not part of Your path or plan for me, so let Your Word remain in me as I REMAIN in You.

God has promised that if you remain in Him, He will remain in you. When He is within you, you gain access to His fruit, His will, and His way. What would your life look like if you chose to remain in Him?

CONSTANT IN PRAYER

Rejoice in hope, be patient in tribulation,
be constant in prayer.

ROMANS 12:12, ESV

I name this day CONSTANT IN PRAYER—not the kind where I hand God a list or tell Him what I think He should do. Not hand-wringing. Not artificial. Not religious language. I step into the kind of prayer that glorifies and elevates You, God, acknowledges Your majesty, is filled with thanksgiving and praise. Pours out my heart, empties my soul, and renews my spirit. When I view it as an active conversation with One my soul loves, I become CONSTANT IN PRAYER.

What does your prayer look like? Are you sending up lists of ailments or problems for God to solve, or are you spending time in active conversation with Him? You can talk to Him like you do your closest friend. Strip away all of the pretenses and just be constant in prayer.

UNDER THE SHADOW

Those who live in the shelter of the Most High
will find rest in the shadow of the Almighty.

PSALM 91:1, NLT

I name this day UNDER THE SHADOW. I choose to dwell in the secret place to fellowship with God. I take shelter beneath His wings. I will abide here with the Almighty. Here I am protected, and I find rest UNDER THE SHADOW.

There is rest to be found under the shadow of the Almighty! Wherever you find yourself today, take a moment to exist in His shadow. It will refresh, renew, and restore you!

YOU LIFT MY HEAD

But in the depths of my heart I truly know that You,
Yahweh, have become my Shield; You take me and surround
me with Yourself. Your glory covers me continually.
You lift high my head when I bow low in shame.

PSALM 3:3, TPT

I name this day YOU LIFT MY HEAD. I can come to You with anything—nothing shocks You or takes You by surprise. You are my shield from enemies, from elements, from myself. Even when I feel unworthy or lost, even when I bow low in shame, You surround me with Yourself.

In Your presence, I am bathed in mercy and covered in glory. You cup my chin in Your hand, and so I might meet Your gaze and see the love and acceptance in Your eyes, YOU LIFT MY HEAD.

Where you see the scars the world has left on you, God sees beauty. When you bow low in shame, regret, or self-loathing, God covers you with His glory and you are made new! Let Him lift your head today. Look up and behold His loving gaze.

NOT GIVING UP

Though he may stumble, he will not fall,
for the LORD upholds him with His hand.

PSALM 37:24, NIV

I name this day NOT GIVING UP. Even when things feel out of control and the odds are stacked against me, I know God is at work. His grace is covering me—like a cocoon covers a caterpillar in the transition to become a butterfly. Surrounded. Protected. Nurtured. Inside God's grace I am still, motionless while He works a miracle. This is just for a little while—Jehovah Sneaky is up to something. He is party planning His lavish celebration for when I emerge transformed. I will look ahead with hope, knowing that the finished work is His plan for me. I'm NOT GIVING UP!

It's perfectly natural to want to fight or flee when the world is stacked against you. However, God asks you to rest in His grace while He orchestrates your miracle. What is it that you might need to cease crying out for rescue and embrace the transition process? Don't give up!

FEAST OF FAVOR

*For the Lord alone is my Savior. What a feast of favor
and bliss He gives His people! Pause in His presence.*

PSALM 3:8, TPT

I name this day FEAST OF FAVOR. Over and over, I run to You, God;
not just in times of trouble but also in seasons of gladness and
joy. You are my True Hero—on dark nights as well as at dawn's
breaking, in troubled waters and on calm seas. Always there.
Today as I pause in Your presence. I am most grateful to be given a
seat at Your FEAST OF FAVOR.

*God invites you to come and dine at His feast of favor. Because He is
your Father, you are eternally invited to His table! Where do you most
need favor today? Close your eyes and picture yourself sitting down at
His table. Now, step into that lavish abundance and feast on favor!*

WRAP-AROUND PRESENCE

God, Your wrap-around presence is my Shield.
You bring victory to all who reach out for You.

PSALM 7:10, TPT

I name this day WRAP-AROUND PRESENCE. Envelop me with Your presence, God. Like a blanket. Like a veil. Like a cloud. As a shield, cover me. I reach out to You, bring me victory! May my thoughts, my words, and my songs be filtered, infused, and overshadowed by Your WRAP-AROUND PRESENCE.

Are you inviting God into the intimate areas of your life, or are you keeping Him at a distance? He wishes to wrap Himself around you, to protect you in every corner of your world. Invite God to envelop you in His wrap-around presence today.

CANDID CONVERSATIONS

Your Father knows what you need before you ask Him.

MATTHEW 6:8, NIV

I name this day CANDID CONVERSATIONS. When I approach You, I need no religious language, no formal protocol, no list. Instead, I come with an unmasked heart, genuine gratitude, deep respect, and no veil. Before I confess, before I lament, before I ask, You already know. What a relief to spend time in the very presence of Love where I have the freedom to engage in CANDID CONVERSATIONS.

Before you even tell Him, God knows your every need, every desire, and every hurt. He invites you to strip away the formality, the "rules," and just be real with Him in your prayers. Clear communication and candid conversations are necessary for every healthy relationship. Talk with God this way today.

KINGDOM AND RIGHTEOUSNESS

But seek first His kingdom and His righteousness
and all these things will be given to you as well.

MATTHEW 6:33, NIV

I name this day KINGDOM AND RIGHTEOUSNESS. I pause and set these things in my heart. Like a detective studies a subject to obtain clues and patterns in order to track them down, this is my approach to "seek first." To learn about an artist, I study his paintings. To know an architect, I study his buildings. God, I want the full background on You. I want to explore and discover everything available to me about You. I am on a steady, relentless pursuit of Your KINGDOM AND RIGHTEOUSNESS.

What do you "seek first?" Are you chasing people or things, or are you on a relentless pursuit to discover more of God? Allow yourself to ask, explore, and to seek first His Kingdom and righteousness. He will reveal it to you.

HEAD ABOVE ALL

*Yours, O Lord, is the greatness and the power and the
glory and the victory and the majesty, for all that is
in the heavens and in the earth is Yours. Yours is the
kingdom, O Lord, and You are exalted as head above all.*

1 CHRONICLES 29:11, ESV

I name this day HEAD ABOVE ALL. You, God, are Lord of Creation, the true and only Master of the Universe. Your glory is displayed everywhere I look. The throne room of nature is more opulent than any palace created by man. I pause in Your presence, breathe in your majesty, and throw my arms wide with praise, shouting, "You are HEAD ABOVE ALL!"

Consider everything that you set your eyes, thoughts, and heart upon. God constantly orchestrates His work for your good, and He alone is in control of the Universe. God is the head above all. Take time to breathe Him in today and experience His glory, victory, majesty, and power.

PRIVATE VICTORIES

"For the LORD your God is going with you!
He will fight for you against your enemies,
and He will give you victory!"

DEUTERONOMY 20:4, NLT

I name this day PRIVATE VICTORIES. It is my secret heart and my secret character where I must first become a champion. It is how I act when no one watches that proves my mettle. I want the public person to be an authentic reflection of the private one.

Today I hold my thought life up to the light. I will tend to the important things and not give in to anxiety, fear, or stress. I am a warrior. I overcome. I fight my battles in the secret place, alone with only my Savior as witness. Public victories result from my PRIVATE VICTORIES.

Before you can conquer the world, you have to conquer your heart. In a world where we post pictures of our coffee on public platforms, it is hard to embrace Christ alone as the witness to our private victories. Let Him lead you there. Let Him develop your character in the secret place.

REACH OUT

If you think you are somebody too important
to stoop down to help another (when really
you are not), you are living in deception.

GALATIANS 6:3, TPT

I name this day REACH OUT. To the weary, the struggling, the falling behind—I will call out to them. I give them the dignity of my notice and offer the kindness of encouragement.

It is easier to look inward and focus on my needs, disappointments, or frustrations. The more I look in, the less I look out. So today, God, highlight others to me. Let me be Your hands and feet, Your mouthpiece on the earth. Today, I will REACH OUT.

It is easy to become distracted by all the things on your calendar. It is easy to get caught up in the every-dayness of life and become focused on yourself. It's normal, really. Today practice reaching out. Be mindful to share God's glory and grace with others in everyday interactions!

FORTIFIED

*In the same way you received Jesus our
Lord and Messiah by faith, continue your journey of faith,
progressing further into your union with Him!
Your spiritual roots go deeply into His life as you are
continually infused with strength, encouraged in every
way. For you are established in the faith you have
absorbed and enriched by your devotion to Him!*

COLOSSIANS 2:6-7, TPT

I name this day FORTIFIED. When I am strong, I am bold. When I know who I am, I am confident. When I am challenged to do so, I grow and this is how I become established.

I will invigorate someone today. I will lend them my energy and creativity. I will strengthen their mind, build them up, bring increase to their courage, and embolden their spirit. As I fortify myself, may others around me become FORTIFIED.

We are meant to progress in our faith. We must nurture spiritual growth to be infused with strength and remain fortified. It is our rich devotion to God that establishes us. From this place, we cannot help but challenge others to know this bounty. Who can you fortify today?

PROTECTED

The Lord is my rock, my fortress and my deliverer;
my God is my rock, in whom I take refuge,
my shield and the horn of my salvation,
my stronghold. I called to the Lord, who is worthy of
praise, and I have been saved from my enemies.

PSALM 18:2-3, NIV

I name this day PROTECTED. I am surrounded by angel armies. God is my deliverer, my rock, my sword, and my shield. He is my salvation and my stronghold. Nothing ... absolutely *nothing* can touch me that has not been "Father-filtered."

God, I stand behind Your shield. You are my fortress and strong tower. You are my help in times of trouble. You train my hands for war. Your grace is sufficient for me. The enemy's arrows may fly in my direction, but I call to You and I am saved from all my enemies. I am PROTECTED.

When you declare God as your fortress and deliverer, strength pours into your heart. Stand confidently behind Him as your shield, call to Him for help, know that He saves you from your enemies. God is your rock—run to Him!

READY FOR ANYTHING

*I know now how to live when things are difficult and
I know how to live when things are prosperous. In
general and in particular I have learned the secret of
facing either poverty or plenty. I am ready for anything
through the strength of the one who lives within me.*

PHILIPPIANS 4:12-13, PHILLIPS

I name this day READY FOR ANYTHING. I can do all things when I allow Christ to strengthen me. I can do things I have never done before, things I have only limited knowledge of, or experience with will unfold before me with supernatural ability. I can abound in prosperity or in difficult hours. I embrace all these possibilities with optimism and confidence.

Today I connect with the resources of heaven and the supernatural power of God to perform. I accept the challenge with a bold confidence that because He lives in me, I am READY FOR ANYTHING.

Feeling overwhelmed, underqualified, or not up to the challenge is common. But Christ lives in you! You can access His strength, His promises, His resources, His purposes, and His plans. Reframe your attitude through this lens and today you will be ready for anything!

RECALIBRATE

Now it's time to change your ways!
Turn to face God so He can wipe away your sins,
pour out showers of blessing to refresh you,
and send you the Messiah
He prepared for you, namely, Jesus.

ACTS 3:19, MSG

I name this day RECALIBRATE. Life can get me off track through regular the everyday challenges. Life can really get me out of whack through forced transitions or trauma.

Today I dare to change the way I think and act. I will face what is out of alignment or threatening my balance. I will look at it straight in the face, find language to describe its damage, and decide to make the necessary adjustments to bring peace, order, and forward momentum back into play. Today I RECALIBRATE.

RECALIBRATE: the act of calibration; to
determine the deviation from a standard so as
to ascertain the proper correction factors, then
adjust for a particular function.

The path to order is paved with awareness and the determination to change. What is out of alignment in your life? In what areas do you need to address and adjust the ways you think and act?

REINFORCEMENTS

He said, "Don't worry about it—
there are more on our side than on their side."
Then Elisha prayed, "O God,
open his eyes and let him see."
The eyes of the young man were opened and he
saw. A wonder! The whole mountainside full of
horses and chariots of fire surrounding Elisha!

2 KINGS 6:16-17 MSG

I name this day REINFORCEMENTS. I call them in. I will answer when called.

There is a heavenly host at the ready. When my focus is on what is greater—the assignment—and not on the personal trial which results or the cost of the sacrifice, then I am positioned to summon the angels to my aid. I stand shoulder to shoulder with my brothers in arms and decree REINFORCEMENTS.

God is for you! He has equipped you for every good work and works for you through every test and trial. You are not alone, His angel armies are with you. Intentionally focus on the big picture today. How can you keep eternity in your gaze?

BELIEF

*Remember this and stand firm, recall it to mind, you
transgressors, remember the former things of old;
for I am God, and there is no other; I am God, and there
is none like Me, declaring the end from the beginning
and from ancient times things not yet done,
saying, "My counsel shall stand, and I will accomplish
all My purpose," calling a bird of prey from the
east, the man of My counsel from a far country.
I have spoken, and I will bring it to pass;
I have purposed, and I will do it.*

ISAIAH 46:8-11, ESV

I name this day BELIEF. I refuse to rehearse the lies of the enemy, I will stand on the Word and acknowledge all I know to be true.

I decree God's plans for me are good. They promise me a future and a hope. His counsel will stand and He will accomplish all that He has purposed. He knows my end from the beginning so I can surely trust Him with the middle! My faith and my hope are activated by my BELIEF.

What do you believe? About God? About yourself? About yourself in relationship to God? What you believe about God is fundamental to every other thing in your life. Examine your heart. Test it. Does what you say you believe align with your practice and confession?

INCREASED CAPACITY

He (Jabez) was the one who prayed to the God of Israel,
"Oh, that you would bless me and expand my territory!
Please be with me in all that I do, and keep me from all
trouble and pain!" And God granted him his request.

1 CHRONICLES 4:10, NLT

I name this day INCREASED CAPACITY. Flexibility is gained through stretching.

I decree more today. More love, more compassion, more wisdom, more understanding. Enlarge my territory and expand my mind. May today be one of INCREASED CAPACITY.

CAPACITY: a mental, emotional, or physical
ability; the potential for treating, experiencing,
or appreciating.

Do you dare to pray a prayer for enlarged territory? Increased capacity? This is a bold prayer wrapped in trust and standing in faith. The stretching of enlargement is worth the blessing of increase. Are you ready to step into more?

STRATEGIC

When you're feeling lazy,
come and learn a lesson from this tale of the tiny ant.
Yes, all you lazybones, come learn
from the example of the ant and enter into wisdom.
The ants have no chief, no boss, no manager—
no one has to tell them what to do.
You'll see them working and toiling all summer long,
stockpiling their food in preparation for winter.

PROVERBS 6:6-8, TPT

I name this day STRATEGIC. I commit my works to the Lord so my plans will be succeed. I will respond to His will and guidance.

A great life isn't lived by accident, it requires intention. Today I step back, assess, regroup and make time to hear from the Lord. It is a season to move with greater intention. I must prepare today for the opportunities I desire tomorrow. I will take more careful steps, and be STRATEGIC.

How often do you rush ahead with plans before seeking the counsel of God's Word and the guidance of His Holy Spirit? Purpose in your heart to become more strategic. What work do you need to commit to Him today?

INTENTIONAL COMPASSION

*But if anyone has the world's goods and sees
his brother in need, yet closes his heart against
him, how does God's love abide in him?*

1 JOHN 3:17, ESV

I name this day INTENTIONAL COMPASSION. I will open my heart to those around me and give them the dignity of being noticed and the kindness of being engaged.

I am the arms of God to someone. When I speak, I whisper His voice to them. When I love, it is His love touching them. Today I will practice INTENTIONAL COMPASSION.

It is easy to get caught up with our responsibilities. The "To-Do" list dictates where our focus, energy, and resources are spent. Today, ask God to highlight someone to you for whom you can be His hands and feet.

BEYOND THE CONTRADICTION

I admit that I haven't yet acquired the absolute fullness that I'm pursuing, but I run with passion into His abundance so that I may reach the purpose for which Christ Jesus laid hold of me to make me His own. I don't depend on my own strength to accomplish this; however I do have one compelling focus: I forget all of the past as I fasten my heart to the future instead.

PHILIPPIANS 3:12-13, TPT

I name this day BEYOND THE CONTRADICTION. I know my identity. I know my calling. I know God's plans for me are good.

Therefore, I press through the circumstances which contradict truth. Facts change, truth remains. I decree circumstances to align with destiny as I choose to agree with God and faithfully and faith-filled-ly press BEYOND THE CONTRADICTION.

What you focus on becomes magnified. If your focus is on your present circumstances, they may contradict the truth of God's promises for you. So, press toward the mark for the prize of the high calling. Fasten your heart to the future and live beyond the contradition!

SEPTEMBER

You're only truly happy when you walk in total integrity,
walking in the light of God's Word.
What joy overwhelms everyone who keeps the ways of God,
those who seek Him as their heart's passion!
They'll never do what's wrong
but will always choose the paths of the Lord.

PSALM 119:1-3, TPT

MARVELOUS

*But those who embraced Him
and took hold of His name,
He gave authority to become the children of God!*

JOHN 1:12, TPT

I name this day MARVELOUS! Clothed in flesh, Jesus made a way for me to have a relationship with Almighty God—to have life, and life abundantly.

Because of His adoption, I am fit to stand before kings, to be part of the priesthood, to communicate with saints. Today I have joy unspeakable and full of glory! How wonderful, how MARVELOUS!

Have you pondered the miracle that Jesus has brought you to the Father? Father God has given you His name—grafted you into the vine, made you His child and a co-heir with His son, Jesus! Though elementary to the faith, this simple truth is astounding. Pause today and ponder this marvel!

HIDDEN TREASURES

The kingdom of heaven is like a treasure hidden in the field,
which a man found and hid again; and from joy over it he
goes and sells everything that he has, and buys that field.

MATTHEW 13:44, NASB

I name this day HIDDEN TREASURES. I will search them out. I will seek out the deep things and explore the height, depth, and breadth of God's goodness.

I decree "finder's keepers" with what I discover today. It is mine. I will possess it to the fullest, take ownership, and joyfully claim all God has for me in this season. Today, I am on the alert and will diligently seek out HIDDEN TREASURES.

Did you ever go on a treasure hunt as a child? Did you ever hide treasures for someone else to find? There is joy in the hiding as well as in the seeking and finding. God wants you to search Him. He has hidden many gems for you to discover, and your joy at finding them delights His heart. Go on a treasure hunt with Him today!

PATIENCE

*But that's not all! Even in times of trouble we have a joyful
confidence, knowing that our pressures will develop in us
patient endurance. And patient endurance will refine our
character, and proven character leads us back to hope.*

ROMANS 5:3-4, TPT

I name this day PATIENCE. Endurance has its perfect reward.
Perseverance is part of the process to succeed.

Today I speak blessings over seeds I have sown, over actions I have
taken, and over habits I have carefully developed. I will not give up;
I will not be discouraged. I press toward the mark for the prize of
the high calling of God in Christ Jesus. Pressure is a gift. It develops
endurance in me. I will stay the course. I will persist for the fruitful
promised, hopeful reward of PATIENCE.

*Challenges stink. But opportunities are wrapped inside them. We
grow most when under pressure. Testing proves us. Strengthens us.
Matures us in ways that allow developed character to sustain us when
promotion comes. What challenge do you need to reframe in the light
of an opportunity?*

TANGIBLE PRESENCE

*Now, may the Lord himself, the Lord of peace, pour into
you His peace in every circumstance and in every possible
way. The Lord's tangible presence be with you all.*

2 THESSALONIANS 3:16, TPT

I name this day TANGIBLE PRESENCE. When all the world is in a tempest, God is my calming force. He surrounds me with His love, and I am sheltered. He pours His peace into me.

I declare steadiness today, tranquility of mind and spirit, humor, mirth, gentleness, peace, and a glad heart. I am Your servant, You are with me. You help me. You strengthen me. You uphold me with Your righteous right hand. I live in the very center of Your TANGIBLE PRESENCE.

Standing as a child of God sometimes leaves you feeling isolated in your convictions or practices. Identifying with Christ sometimes means getting lumped into a people group with character very different from your own. Stand anyway. God is with you. He knows your name and has called you His own. When the storm rages, you can be calm.

SEPTEMBER 5

UNITY

*Whatever happens, keep living your lives based on the
reality of the Gospel of Christ. Then when I come to
see you, or hear good reports of you, I'll know that you
stand united in one Spirit and one passion—celebrating
together as conquerors in the faith of the Gospel.*

PHILIPPIANS 1:27, TPT

I name this day UNITY. All the pieces are here—nothing is missing.
Our unique representations are beautiful, but fashioned to function
as the expression of Christ in the earth. Help me see the vision for
the whole picture and trust that You will piece it together.

I block confusion. I release love—enough love to drown out fear
that stirs up strife and threatens to keep us divided. We are Your
church. We are one. More unites us than divides us if only we
will find it and nurture its growth. Work the miracle of binding us
together with unbreakable cords. God, restore us in UNITY.

*UNITY: a way of combining parts in a work of
art or literature so that they belong together.*

*Unity pleases God. When we operate in unity, power and glory are
released in the earth. Pray today for unity. Pray for the church. Ask God
to work a miracle as only He can and allow His body to experience the
beautiful bonds of unity.*

PERFECT PEACE

*Thou wilt keep him in perfect peace, whose mind
is stayed on Thee: because he trusteth in Thee.*

ISAIAH 26:3, KJV

I name this day PERFECT PEACE. I release it into the earth. I release it into my heart. I understand that peace is not the absence of something, but the presence of Someone.

I embrace the Prince of Peace. I will walk in honor, demonstrate understanding, and show kindness. I decree civility, respect, and empathy over my community, and I will lead the way. My mind is stayed on You, God, and You keep me in PERFECT PEACE.

You've got peace like a river! Even when there is conflict, you have access to the Prince of Peace. Give Him your mind. Hand Him your anxieties and cares. Today, make a list of people and situations over which you need to release peace. Speak this out loud and watch what God will do!

UNSHEATHED

"If anyone dares to stir up strife against you, it is not from Me! Those who challenge you will go down in defeat. See, I am the one who created the craftsman who fans the coals into a fire and forges a weapon fit for its purpose, and I am the one who created the destroyer to destroy. But I promise you, no weapon meant to hurt you will succeed, and you will refute every accusing word spoken against you. This promise is the inheritance of Yahweh's servants, and their vindication is from Me," says Yahweh.

ISAIAH 54:15-17, TPT

I name this day UNSHEATHED. I will pull out my weapon from the place where it rests and wield it with skill. I am equipped. I have been trained. My mind is well conditioned, and I am fit for fight! I declare no weapon formed against me shall prosper. I will not sit still and passively yield to the pressures of the onslaught. Enemy be warned, today my sword is sharpened and UNSHEATHED.

UNSHEATHED: to uncover a weapon, to draw it from its protective coating so it ready for use.

The Lord fights for us. This is such good news! There are times, however, when we are called to stand firm while wearing the full armor of God and wielding the sword of the Spirit against our enemies. Is your weapon ready? Are you in battle position? Pick up your sword—God goes before you!

BROAD SHOULDERS

If anyone sees a fellow believer in need and has the means
to help him, yet shows no pity and closes his heart against
him, how is it even possible that God's love lives in him?

1 JOHN 3:17, TPT

I name this day BROAD SHOULDERS. Because God allows me to place my burdens on Him, I am empowered to stand and help shoulder the burdens of others.

I release compassion today—the kind that comes when you stand arm and arm, shoulder to shoulder, to dry tears and love beyond any capacity you imagined possible. I stand with supernatural compassion for those who are weary of heart. I bring comfort to those grieving and in need of a tangible connection to God's BROAD SHOULDERS.

It takes supernatural strength to step into the comfort of God in such a way that we become that tangible expression to someone else. God created us to bear one another's burdens and carry each other's troubles. Who in your life needs that kind of compassion from you today?

263

I WIN

Now thanks be to God who always
leads us in triumph in Christ ...

2 CORINTHIANS 2:14a, NKJV

I name this day I WIN. I move through life knowing I am already victorious. I will win because in Christ the matter is already settled; I have already won!

I step into the completed work of faith today. I step into the reality of "It is finished," and I know I am victorious. I decree victory. I declare strategy coming forth that takes me on a path which agrees the completed work of victory. I WIN!

Say this out loud: "Thanks be to God who ALWAYS causes me to TRIUMPH!" Step into the place of "already done" and operate today in the faith of the finished work. Positionally, you have already won. Now activate your faith for that victory to manifest.

PROPEL

For I will turn toward you [with favor and regard]
and make you fruitful and multiply you, and I will
establish and confirm My covenant with you.

LEVITICUS 26:9, AMP

I name this day PROPEL. I feel the force of favor behind me like the swelling of an ocean wave. There is a tide of triumph breaking over me. God has turned toward me. He makes me fruiful, and I will multiply!

I decree momentum behind my destiny. I decree acceleration in the accomplishment of key goals and objectives. I feel rocket fuel in my tank, the afterburners have kicked in, and into my spirit I speak the word PROPEL!

PROPEL: to cause to move forward or onward.

Receive God's energy today. Pause and ponder His covenant with you, the gifts and talents He has given you, and the promises Has has made you. Feel His favor. Receive His regard. Now, drink in that flow of favor and allow it to propel you in the direction of your God-dream.

ANSWERS

With all my might I shout up to God,
His answers thunder from the holy mountain.

PSALM 3:4, MSG

I name this day ANSWERS. I am shielded on all sides, my feet are grounded, and my head is lifted high. I can ask You any question God. I can hand You my anger, disappointments, doubts, and frustrations. You do not want me to hide my confusion from You. You do not want me to seek answers from other sources when my questioning seems "not religious enough" to approach you.

You promise that when I shout up to You, thunder from Your holy mountain will send forth to me ANSWERS!

There are questions that seem too disrespectful to ask God. Admitting you feel hurt by God or disappointed in Him seems almost blasphemous. So, we pretend we aren't in an attempt to stay "right with God." I promise, He can handle it. God wants you to come to Him with any and everything on your heart. What do you need to ask God about today?

HARVEST

*Now may He who supplies seed to the sower, and
bread for food, supply and multiply the seed you have
sown and increase the fruits of your righteousness.*

2 CORINTHIANS 9:10, NKJV

I name this day HARVEST. I will reap in due season. I will faint not.

I decree every seed I have sown in faith will reproduce after its kind. I declare a hundred fold return for faithful seeds planted in fertile soil. I bless my harvest. I will not curse it, belittle it, or corrupt it by careless words or expectations. Today I say, "Come forth, HARVEST!"

> *FOLD RETURN: representative of all the increase potential
> in a single seed—that tree and all its fruit, and all the trees
> and fruit from the seeds that tree yeilds. A fold return
> indicates multiplication of harvest too numerous to count.
> It is generational and perpetual.*

*Harvest is a beautiful rhythm of life. It is one of God's laws—seedtime
and harvest. What we sow, we reap. Sometimes we faint before a seed
has its season. Sometimes we dig it up and destroy it before it has
the chance to bear fruit. What seed do you have in the ground? What
harvest are you believing for?*

WORDS WELL SPOKEN

So shall My word be that goes forth from My mouth;
it shall not return to Me void,
but it shall accomplish what I please,
and it shall prosper in the thing for which I sent it.

ISAIAH 55:11, NKJV

I name this day WORDS WELL SPOKEN. I will purposefully and intentionally watch over my tongue, realizing every word I speak is a seed that bears fruit after its own kind.

I command my words to go and grow. They are like soldiers I send out into the universe bearing my authority to complete the task for which I have assigned it. I commit today to speak only WORDS WELL SPOKEN.

Your words are powerful. God created the universe with His words! Your words craft the world in which you live. They shape your reality. What words have you been releasing over your life? Your health? Your relationships? Your finances? Purpose today to become intentional and make sure your words are well spoken.

LEVEL UP

To this He replied, "You cannot know times and dates which have been fixed by the Father's sole authority. But you are to be given power when the Holy Spirit has come to you. You will be witnesses to Me, not only in Jerusalem, not only throughout Judea, not only in Samaria, but to the very ends of the earth!"

ACTS 1:8, PHILLIPS

I name this day LEVEL UP! I showed up, not knowing I had been set up for a level up. I'm going higher, pressing farther, believing bigger, reaching for more, wanting all that's in store.

Process is for my protection. Pain has polished my character. Refined. Renewed. Empowered. Imbued. I surrender to dreams larger than mine. I say yes to You, God, ready to embrace all that will be required of me as I LEVEL UP.

IMBUED: inspired and permeated with a feeling or quality; to introduce one thing into another so as to affect it throughout.

Sometimes what feels like a setback is actually a set up. Nothing can touch you that has not first been filtered by God's sovereignty. He has promised to give you power through the Holy Spirit. That power equips you for whatever He asks of you. Are you ready to level up?

MIRACLES

And to another, the same Spirit gives the gift of faith.
And to another, the same Spirit gives gifts of healing.
And to another the power to work miracles ...

1 CORINTHIANS 12:9-10a, TPT

I name this day MIRACLES. God comes through! Today I expect nothing but favor, grace, and provision in both the natural and the spiritual realms.

God, show me Your wonders. Show me Your goodness. Teach me to walk in Your ways. I believe. I believe in Your mighty power. I believe in the resurrection and stand in awe at the wonderous work of redemption and restoration to my heart. God, I believe in MIRACLES!

Do you believe God still works miracles today? Not just for other people, but for you? Stretch your faith toward God today. Boldly approach His throne in reverence and in awe and ask Him to show you His wonders. Ask Him to reveal His goodness to you. Ask Him to let you witness a miracle!

PLEASANT PATH

Yahweh, You alone are my inheritance.
You are my prize, my pleasure, and my portion.
You hold my destiny and its timing in Your hands.
Your pleasant path leads me to pleasant places.
I'm overwhelmed by the privileges
that come with following You!

PSALM 16:5-6, TPT

I name this day PLEASANT PATH. The Lord is my portion and my cup, He makes my lot secure. The boundary lines have fallen for me in pleasant places and I have a delightful inheritance!

I decree favorable agreements and arrangements today. I declare total security in the Lord. Because He cares about the details of my life, I can rest totally secure. Because of His great love for me, this day, I walk along a PLEASANT PATH.

God holds your destiny and the timing of its unfolding in His hands. Sometimes the path is filled with peace, and sometimes it is cluttered with burdens and obstacles. His promise, though, is that He will lead you to pleasant places. Let Him guide you along that path today.

SEPTEMBER 17

OPPORTUNITY

*... All the bridesmaids got up and prepared their lamps.
Then the five foolish ones asked the others, "Please give
us some of your oil because our lamps are going out."
But the others replied, "We don't have enough for all
of us. Go to a shop and buy some for yourselves."
But while they were gone to buy oil, the bridegroom
came. Then those who were ready went in with
him to the marriage feast, and the door was
locked. ... "So you, too, must keep watch! For you
do not know the day or hour of My return."*

SEE MATTHEW 25:1-13, NLT

I name this day OPPORTUNITY. I will diligently prepare for the opportunities I desire in my future. When it comes, I will be ready.

I heighten my awareness and place myself on the alert to recognize opportunity when it crosses my path. I expect them to manifest. I challenge myself to faithfully, boldly, and confidently act when I encounter a God-ordained OPPORTUNITY.

Opportunity meets preparation. What opportunities are you desiring? If it showed up today, would you be ready to engage it? If not, what steps do you need to take today to begin preparing for the opportunity you seek tomorrow?

272

TRUTH

Then you will know the truth,
and the truth will set you free.

JOHN 8:32, NIV

I name this day TRUTH. To be set free requires that I know and embrace truth. Today I swing my arms wide and open my heart to receive truth.

Wherever I encounter captivity—in my mind or in the minds of others—may I bring truth to the situation. I will wrap truth in love, clothe it in compassion, and bring it with mercy and grace, but without fail, I will loose truth. I decree my spirit to abide in truth today. I intentionally fill my heart with the Word of God and seek to know the One who is TRUTH.

A paraphrased line from a popular television show said, "The truth will set you free, but first it will make you mad." When truth confronts the lies we have believed, it can be hard to let the lie go. But truth—what God says about you—is a path to freedom like no other. Where do you need to embrace truth today?

SUCCESSION

But you are a chosen generation, a royal priesthood,
a holy nation, His own special people, that you
may proclaim the praises of Him who called you
out of darkness into His marvelous light.

1 PETER 2:9, NKJV

I name this day SUCCESSION. I will prepare my heart to receive the mantle of authority God has established for me. I align my desires with His purpose.

I am aware that things lawful for others are not profitable for me. Because of the weight of my calling, I will command my character to come up higher. I decree that I am rooted and grounded in the Word of God. As I abound unto every good work. I am a priest and a king, stepping into my SUCCESSION.

Understanding the difference between what is lawful and what is profitable is foundational to spiritual growth. It is wisdom with understanding. You are a royal priesthood—a king and a priest. In what ways are you holding your character accountable to your calling?

UNPLUGGED

*There was such a swirl of activity around Jesus,
with so many people coming and going, that they
were unable to even eat a meal. So Jesus said to
His disciples, "Come, let's take a break and find a
secluded place where you can rest a while."*

MARK 6:31, TPT

I name this day UNPLUGGED. Today I will pull away and unplug from distractions, unplug from cares and worries. I will rest—my body, my mind, my soul.

The Sabbath was made for man and not man for the Sabbath. God put the principle of the Sabbath in place for my good. He wants me to rest. He wants me to return to Him and be filled, replenished, and renewed. I choose to embrace this provision and, therefore, today I will remain UNPLUGGED.

Rest is a strategy. Time away from cutting to sharpen your axe will allow you to cut more with less energy expended. Take a break. Even if you must schedule it, spend some time alone in seclusion where you can be restored. Rest.

FUTURE

*And we articulate these realities with the words imparted
to us by the Spirit and not with the words taught by
human wisdom. We join together Spirit-revealed truths
with Spirit-revealed words. Someone living on an entirely
human level rejects the revelations of God's Spirit, for
they make no sense to him. He can't understand the
revelations of the Spirit because they are only discovered
by the illumination of the Spirit. Those who live in the
Spirit are able to carefully evaluate all things, and
they are subject to the scrutiny of no one but God.*

1 CORINTHIANS 2:13-15, TPT

I name this day FUTURE. I see who I want to become, and I will actively and intentionally come into agreement with that image. I will speak this over myself and pursue a course that molds me in that direction until my circumstances no longer contradict my vision for the future.

First, I see it; then I'll say it until I become it. I decree favor, divine connections, and increased faith for this pursuit. I command my reality to line up with my face in the FUTURE.

"We articulate these realities with the words imparted to us by the Spirit and not with the words taught by human wisdom." What realities is God speaking to you regarding your future. Give these words utterance. Write them down. Meditate on them. Speak them over yourself and step into what He has for you!

WALLS

But now I said to them, "You know very well what
trouble we are in. Jerusalem lies in ruins, and its
gates have been destroyed by fire. Let us rebuild
the wall of Jerusalem and end this disgrace!"
Then I told them about how the gracious hand of God had
been on me, and about my conversation with the king.
They replied at once, "Yes, let's rebuild the
wall!" So they began the good work.

NEHEMIAH 2:16-18, TPT

I name this day WALLS. I will rule over my own spirit. I will exercise restraint. I am committed to developing the character of Christ in my life. I willingly submit my nature to His; I bow my will to His design.

I decree the words of my mouth and my meditation become acceptable in God's sight. Like Nehemiah, I choose to fortify my city, I repair her gates, and I rebuild the WALLS.

City walls represent protection. They symbolize the strength of a city, and the God they serve. Gates are the access points. They represent vulnerability and strategy. You are a city set on a hill, and your life also has walls and gates. What is the condition of your walls?

SEPTEMBER 23

NEW

If you have heard Jesus and have been taught by Him according to the truth that is in Him, then you know to take off your former way of life, your crumpled old self—that dark blot of a soul corrupted by deceitful desire and lust—to take a fresh breath and to let God renew your attitude and spirit. Then you are ready to put on your new self, modeled after the very likeness of God: truthful, righteous, and holy.

EPHESIANS 4:21-24, VOICE

I name this day NEW. I am a new creation in Christ. The old has passed away, and the new has come. I choose to no longer dwell on former things but to let the new thing spring forth out of the wilderness.

I will not rehearse, revisit, or rehash what has been put under the Blood of the Lamb, washed, and made clean. I will focus instead on His purpose, His promise, His provision, and His plan. When the sun rises each day, it brings with it mercies that are NEW.

What a blessing that God constructed the earth's rotation and calendar to allow us seasons and the passing of time. Endings. Beginnings. Newness. What do you need to let go of from a past season? What needs to pass away in order for fresh, new things to spring forth in your life?

KINDNESS

Do you have contempt for God, who is very kind to you,
puts up with you, and deals patiently with you?
Don't you realize that it is God's kindness that is trying to
lead you to Him and change the way you think and act?

ROMANS 2:4, GW

I name this day KINDNESS. I choose kindness. It is God's kindness that leads me to repentance. His kindness removes every false filter and cushion that lies between me and Him.

So, it will be the kindness of God working through me that might open a heart to be drawn to Him. For sure, if I am not operating in kindness, I have no hope of representing Him well.

Today I will be intentionally kind. I will check my words before I speak to them to make sure God's voice can be heard through them. Because God is kind, I will put on KINDNESS.

Don't confuse being nice with being kind. Kindness knows what is at stake and loves enough to refuse being a false filter between someone we love and God. God's kindness at work is patient, has eternity in its scope, and does not interfere with or protect from things that would lead a heart to Him. What does kindness look like to you?

RESOLVED

Stand firm, and you will win life.

LUKE 21:19, NIV

I name this day RESOLVED. I declare that the door is shut on old things, and their power to interfere with my thoughts is blocked. I speak resolution to matters that linger and answers to problems. Strategy and solutions will emerge today.

I speak healing balm over raw emotions and invite my soul to rest in the peace of God. The matter is settled. Victory through the storm has been established. Details to wrap it up are becoming clear today, and hope for a new season is kindled into burning flame. I am determined to move forward. I am RESOLVED.

RESOLVED: to settle things successfully,
to reach a firm decision, to go from
dissonance to consonance.

It starts with a decision. What are you resolved to do? What awaits you when you can put past failures and disappointments behind you and begin building a hopeful, positive future. What decision do you need to make today?

RESTORE

*I will restore to you the years that the swarming locust
has eaten, the hopper, the destroyer, and the cutter,
My great army, which I sent among you.
"You shall eat in plenty and be satisfied, and praise the
name of the Lord your God, who has dealt wondrously with
you. And my people shall never again be put to shame.*

JOEL 2:25-26, ESV

I name this day RESTORE. That which is lost, that which has been broken, that which is forgotten, has been abandoned, or is yet to be fulfilled, my prayer today, Lord, is that You will RESTORE.

I release disappointment, surrender discouragement, lay down hurts and broken dreams as I surrender pain and yield my brokenness up to You. Enter my soul today, fill it with joy. Enter my heart and make it clean. Enter my spirit and make it new. Come as only You can and fully RESTORE.

Step into the Shalom of God—nothing missing, nothing broken. God will restore to you all that has been lost. Even that which seems impossible, God invites you into the beautiful mystery of eternity. The hope that He can and will make all things new is a promise worthy of meditation.

GRACIOUS

But You, Lord, are a compassionate and gracious God,
slow to anger, abounding in love and faithfulness.

PSALM 86:15, NIV

I name this day GRACIOUS. It is not always easy because people can be difficult and the do dumb things. You, God abound in love and faithfulness. You are compassionate and slow to anger.

Father, kindle in me this kind of generosity of spirit. Season me with grace—let it flow from me in word, thought, and deed. May Your character cling to me and cause me to be GRACIOUS.

It is hard to be gracious in a rude world. It takes the Father's eyes, the character of Christ, and the power of the Holy Spirit to function with grace in a graceless place. Ask God to help you be mindful today and be a conduit of His grace wherever you go.

HEAVENLY TREASURES

Don't keep hoarding for yourselves earthly treasures
that can be stolen by thieves. Material wealth eventually
rusts, decays, and loses its value. Instead, stockpile
heavenly treasures for yourselves that cannot be
stolen and will never rust, decay, or lose their value.

MATTHEW 6:19-20, TPT

I name this day HEAVENLY TREASURES. Everyday responsibilities and cares are part of life, and attending to them is responsible, wise stewardship. But I focus my eyes on eternity. Today I will weigh my priorities against things that have lasting, eternal value.

I want to store up things I can lay at Your feet, things which cannot be stolen, that will not rust, decay, or lose their value. God, today I will store up HEAVENLY TREASURES.

Matthew exhorts us in this chapter to examine ourselves and make sure what we do is not to show off or gain admiration, but out of our love for God, motivated to bring Him more glory. What kind of things fall into the category of "heavenly treasures"? How can you store these up?

CHEERFUL

A cheerful heart brings a smile to your face;
a sad heart makes it hard to get through the day.

PROVERBS 15:13, MSG

I name this day CHEERFUL. It is a state of mind. It is the happy by-product of gratitude, a symptom of living thankful.

I put aside negativity and embrace hopeful, positive, optimistic possibilities. I will smile on purpose. I hope to be this naturally, but even when challenged, I choose CHEERFUL.

It is okay to have seasons of sadness. But pessimism, negativity, and a sour countenance spoil life. Sometimes cheerfulness requires intentionality. Sometimes we must smile until we feel like smiling. Do you notice areas where you can adopt a more cheerful, hopeful, optimistic approach?

FULL HEART

I'm thanking You, God, from a full heart,
I'm writing the book on Your wonders.
I'm whistling, laughing, and jumping for joy;
I'm singing Your song, High God.

PSALM 9:1, MSG

I name this day FULL HEART. I've got one—full of joy, full of hope, full of gratitude, full of freedom.

This full heart makes my thoughts full of God, my mouth full of praise, and my actions full of love. Yes, today is definitely a FULL HEART day!

I hear a song from my childhood: "I've got the joy, joy, joy, joy down in my heart!" Whenever I can get outside my head long enough to tune into my heart, I find that gratitude fills it with joy. When my heart is full of joy, then I am full of strength. What fills your heart today?

OCTOBER

*That is why my heart is glad and my soul rejoices.
My body rests securely because You do
not abandon my soul to the grave
or allow Your holy one to decay.*

PSALM 16:9-10, GW

APPROACH GOD

Let us therefore approach the throne of grace with fullest confidence, that we may receive mercy for our failures and grace to help in the hour of need.

HEBREWS 4:16, PHILLIPS

I name this day APPROACH GOD. With humility, gratitude, and expectation, I seek God. I knock on the door, and come before His throne of grace. He's a good Father with limitless supply. I am His child, given the access of a beloved favorite. He meets my failure with mercy. He helps me. Therefore, as I stand in His presence, I can confidently and reverently APPROACH GOD.

APPROACH: to draw near, to advance nearer.

There are times when we feels like we must first wash up—clean up our act a bit—before we seek an audience with the King of the Universe. But Jesus has covered us in His righteousness, so we may come before God in any state. Approach God confidently today. His throne of grace awaits you.

VICTORY

The Lord will make you the head and not the tail;
you will only move upward and never downward if
you listen to the Lord your God's commands I am
giving you today and are careful to follow them.

DEUTERONOMY 28:13, CSB

I name this day VICTORY! Thanks be to God who always causes me to win! Through Him I can do all things, I am the head and not the tail, above and not beneath, whatever I put my hand to shall prosper.

Today, no matter what my emotions or circumstances say, I will listen and obey God's commands. In Christ, I already have the VICTORY!

Walking in victory is a choice. When things are sunny-side-up, this is easy, but when there are storm clouds hovering, it is hard to remember that victory is already ours. Today, step into victory. Put on the mind of Christ. Access the finished work of grace and stand your ground. Shout, "I have the victory!"

REHOBOTH

*He moved on from there and dug another well,
and no one quarreled over it. He named it
Rehoboth, saying, "Now the Lord has given us
room and we will flourish in the land."*

GENESIS 26:22, NIV

I name this day REHOBOTH. The Lord has made a place for me without contention, without enmity, and here I will flourish.

I decree a reopening of the wells of my fathers. Access to promised blessing is restored to me and my seed. I draw the blessings up so I can freely pour them out. This is my season of entering REHOBOTH.

*REHOBOTH: (Hebrew) broad places;
open spaces, roomy.*

Genesis 26 is the story of Isaac traveling to Beersheba where the Lord promised to be with him and fulfill His promises to his father, Abraham. He re-dug the wells of his father and made peace with his enemies. What blessings belong to your bloodline? Dig them up. Claim them. Step into the open spaces and flourish!

JOY

So you'll go out in joy,
you'll be led into a whole and complete life.
The mountains and hills will lead the parade,
bursting with song. All the trees of the
forest will join the procession,
exuberant with applause.

ISAIAH 55:12, MSG

I name this day JOY. I sing the song, "Joy, unspeakable joy, the world didn't give it to me ... The world didn't give it, and they can't take it away!"

I release joy today! I coat my soul in non-stick Teflon so negativity will not stick to me. I decree that peace protects my spirit, and everywhere I go, spontaneous joy will follow. I give, I have, I am JOY!

Joy is not a feeling so much as it is a recognition that our state is dependent on who Jesus is, not on who we are or what is happening to or around us. In God's presence, our joy is full, complete. In what ways can you step into and release joy today?

TEACHABLE

Anyone willing to be corrected
is on the pathway to life.
Anyone refusing has lost his chance.

PROVERBS 10:17, TLB

I name this day TEACHABLE. I don't know what I don't know, therefore, I open myself up to learn. With curiosity and humility, I seek to know and experience more.

I am willing to be instructed, willing to be adjusted. I desire to embrace all God has for me, therefore I will remain TEACHABLE.

Are you teachable, or do you get defensive or frustrated when someone points out something you need to correct, adjust, or learn? God's heart for you is that you grow in wisdom, gain knowledge and understanding. Reflect today on how teachable you are. Wherever you are on that scale, purpose to open yourself up to becoming more teachable.

EXTRAVAGANTLY LOVED

*Consider the kind of extravagant love the Father has
lavished on us—He calls us children of God! It's true; we are
His beloved children. And in the same way the world didn't
recognize Him, the world does not recognize us either.*

1 JOHN 3:1, VOICE

I name this day EXTRAVAGANTLY LOVED. Though I don't always
know how to receive this kind of love, and though accepting this
as fact confounds my mind, I reach by faith into this magnificent
promise.

I am astounded that I can be fully known—all my faults, flaws, and
failures, and still be acceptable to God. I gratefully acknowledge
the miracle that I am EXTRAVAGANTLY LOVED.

*God loves you with an extravagant love. He loves you because He is
love, not because you have earned it or deserve it. The One who sees all
and knows all loves you beyond comprehension. Pause in His presence
and let His love wash over you today. Ask Him to reveal His extravagant
love to you today.*

BEAMING

Therefore they shall come and sing in the height of Zion,
streaming to the goodness of the Lord—
for wheat and new wine and oil,
for the young of the flock and the herd;
their souls shall be like a well-watered garden,
and they shall sorrow no more at all.

JEREMIAH 31:12, NKJV

I name this day BEAMING. My face is beaming, radiant from God's bounty.

I step into abundance. I am a well-watered garden. God's goodness surrounds me. He is the source of my supply, never-ending provision, divine appointments, heaven-prepared opportunities. He gives me joy in place of my sorrows. Because of all this, I am BEAMING.

BEAMING: cheeful, bright, radiant.

What is your countenance like? Do you emit the glory and goodness of God, or is your face sour, sad, or weary? Step into God's abundance today. You are a well-watered garden—drink that in. Sing songs of Zion. Celebrate God's goodness and let your countenance reflect His joy in you.

FAITHFUL

He was full of unfailing love and faithfulness.

JOHN 1:14b, NLT

I name this day FAITHFUL. I will firmly adhere to truth, be loyal to those whom I love, exercise fidelity to covenants I have entered. I will celebrate God's faithfulness to me and praise Him for it with gratitude. Remembering the crown of life is at stake, unto death will I be FAITHFUL.

God's faithfulness to us is great. Faithfulness is a fruit of the Spirit (Galatians 5:22). In what ways has God demonstrated His faithfulness to you? In what ways can you demonstrate your faithfulness to Him?

INTO THE LIGHT

*Take no part in the unfruitful works of darkness, but instead
expose them. For it is shameful even to speak of the things
that they do in secret. But when anything is exposed by
the light, it becomes visible, for anything that becomes
visible is light. Therefore it says, "Awake, O sleeper, and
arise from the dead, and Christ will shine on you." Look
carefully then how you walk, not as unwise but as wise,
making the best use of the time, because the days are evil.*

EPHESIANS 5:11-16, ESV

I name this day INTO THE LIGHT. With gratitude and grit, I rejoice
under pressure, I sing through trials, I anticipate the new wine that
comes from the crushing. I do not shrink, waver, or hide, but by
God's grace allow the pressing to squeeze my character until it
becomes exposed—visible, not secret or hidden. God, I welcome
the way You pull me INTO THE LIGHT.

*Because you are fully loved no matter what, you can risk being fully
known. If you desire God's character at work in you, step into the light.
Let Him reveal every area where you need His mercy and grace to cover
and adjust you. What parts of your soul need exposure to God's light
today?*

AMAZED

O Lord, You are my God.
I will highly honor You; I will praise Your name.
You have done miraculous things.
You have been completely reliable
in carrying out Your plans from long ago.

ISAIAH 25:1, GW

I name this day AMAZED. God's greatness is bigger than my faith. The doors He opens lead not just to rooms, but to completely new realms!

I will stand in Your greatness today and refuse to feel small. I will allow myself to encounter You in wonder and in awe. I encourage my heart to explore Your magnitude. I stand AMAZED.

It is easy to lose our sense of awe and wonder. In a world of special effects, psychological thrillers, and science fiction, ordinary life can seem dull and plain. Our faith can feel quaint and old-fashioned. But God is very much alive! He still works wonders. Open your heart and be amazed by the God of creation. Stand in His greatness today.

MOVE

For we walk by faith, not by sight.
2 CORINTHIANS 5:7, NKJV

I name this day MOVE. Because I walk by faith and not by sight, I will not be hindered by not knowing all the steps. I will start with the one right in front of me.

I refuse to be paralyzed by indecision or freeze in my uncertainty. I will instead cast my bread upon the waters. I will heed Your voice and respond to the Spirit's prompting. In faith, I will MOVE.

What action are you hesitant to take because you don't yet know what the outcome will be? Today, ask God to increase your faith so you can move even in uncertainty—trust Him even when you cannot see what is next. What does a step of faith look like for you right now?

PERSISTENT COURAGE

*Have I not commanded you? Be strong and of good
courage; do not be afraid, nor be dismayed, for the
Lord your God is with you wherever you go.*

JOSHUA 1:9, NKJV

I name this day PERSISTENT COURAGE. It is God who gives me strength. I have no cause to fear, no reason to feel anxious or distressed. God goes before me. His angels are my rear guard and protect my flanks.

I am strong in the Lord and in the power of His might. Because God is with me, I can walk in PERSISTENT COURAGE.

Courage is often describe as "doing it afraid" or as strength in the face of grief or pain. When we withstand difficulty, persevere in opposition, and display mental and moral strength, we are said to be courageous. You are not born with courage; it is developed as you go through trials and emerge. Today, be strong. You are courageous.

HELD CLOSE

Even if my father and mother abandon me,
the Lord will hold me close.

PSALM 27:10, NLT

I name this day HELD CLOSE—in my Father's arms, against His chest, hearing His heartbeat, feeling His warmth, and the steady rhythm of His breathing. I cast all my cares, worries, and anxieties on Him. There in His arms I am safe, there I am comforted, there am I HELD CLOSE.

There is no safer place to be than in the arms of the Father. There beneath the shadow of His wing you are protected. There in the palm of His hand, nothing can harm you. Close your eyes. Take a long, deep, slow breath and in that stillness, let Him hold you close.

GREAT PEACE

All your children shall be taught by the Lord,
And great shall be the peace of your children.

ISAIAH 54:13, NKJV

I name this day GREAT PEACE. The seeds I have planted bear fruit and flourish. My children know the Lord and He guides their path. They walk in wisdom and find favor with God and man.

With great hope for their future, and patience to see God bring it to pass, I claim the promise that my children shall be taught by the Lord, and they will have GREAT PEACE.

It can be hard to comprehend God's eternal perspective. Releasing our children to the Lord is an act of extreme trust. He knows their end from their beginning, and His love for them is enduring. Stand on this promise today: all my children shall be taught of the Lord, and great shall be their peace!

LIFTED

For God has not destined us, His chosen, to face His wrath but to be the heirs of salvation through our Lord Jesus the Anointed, the Liberating King, who died for us. So regardless of whether we are awake or asleep, we will live together with Him. So support one another. Keep building each other up as you have been doing.

1 THESSALONIANS 5:9-11, VOICE

I name this day LIFTED. I lift Jesus higher. He is my glory and the lifter of my head. He is my Liberating King!

I offer encouragment. I support others' dreams and goals. I build them up. I am like the tide: when I come in, all boats rise! I am a lifter, and by the buoyancy of my spirit, those around me will also be LIFTED.

How do you show up in a room? What gets left behind in your wake? Your emotional state reflects your spiritual state, and its energy is contagious. Be mindful today of the atmosphere you create. Carry the freedom of the Liberating King in your heart and watch your impact!

THOUGHTFUL

*Finally, brothers and sisters, whatever is true, whatever
is noble, whatever is right, whatever is pure, whatever
is lovely, whatever is admirable—if anything is
excellent or praiseworthy—think about such things.*

PHILIPPIANS 4:8, NIV

I name this day THOUGHTFUL. I will think on things true, noble, right, pure, lovely, admirable, excellent, and praiseworthy.

I will pause to reflect on what I sense the Spirit is saying to me. I will ponder what You whisper to my heart. I will not simply bustle through my busy day, instead I will take the time to enjoy Your presence, to spend time with you and be THOUGHTFUL.

What are you thinking about? What script is looping through your mind? Is it praiseworthy? Is it filled with truth? Awareness and reflection are God's gift to us to declutter our minds and quiet our hearts. Take time today to sit in peace for a few minutes and let your mind dwell on God-breathed things.

DIVE IN

I ponder every morsel of wisdom from You,
I attentively watch how You've done it.
I relish everything You've told me of life,
I won't forget a word of it.

PSALM 119:15-16, MSG

I name this day DIVE IN. I long for the deep things. God, Your riches are unfathomable, incomprehensible ... and completely worth exploring.

Today, I will ponder every morsel of wisdom from You. I want to know more of You, more of Your Word. So today, with rapt attention, faithfully I DIVE IN.

Has something ever grabbed your notice with such intensity that you dropped everything to satisfy your curiosity? What if you approached God's Word with that anticipation? Deep calls unto deep. Grab your spiritual scuba gear and dive in!

GLOW

*For once you were full of darkness, but now you have
light from the Lord. So live as people of light!*

EPHESIANS 5:8, NLT

I name this day GLOW. May the light in me shine brightly. May it spread warmth and joy, may it dispel darkness, and be a beacon of guidance or hope.

"This little light of mine, I'm gonna let it shine ..." God, let the flame in my heart burn with such intensity that every person I encounter will be touched by the warmth of its GLOW.

Christ is the light of the world. His light shines in us and through us, invading the darkness by our witness of Him in the earth. The more you receive of Him, the brighter His light grows within you. Today, I encourage you to glow, baby, glow!

SACRIFICE

*There is no greater love than to lay
down one's life for one's friends.*

JOHN 15:13, NLT

I name this day SACRIFICE. I choose to prefer others in honor. I willingly, freely lay down my life for those I love, expecting nothing in return.

When I am tempted to let someone know the effort or cost involved in demonstrating my love, I will remember that comes from a selfish desire and relinquish that need for credit or approval. Because I desire to love like Jesus, I embrace SACRIFICE.

*SACRIFICE: a thing surrendered or given up
for the sake of obtaining something (such as
peace) or helping someone else.*

There are many things worth sacrificing for. The people God has placed in your life and are in your circle of influence are worthy of investment. Reframe sacrifices made for them as worship unto Him. It is service rendered to God for His beloved. Take joy that He sees all and knows the price you have paid.

PROMOTION

This I know: the favor that brings promotion and power
doesn't come from anywhere on earth,
for no one exalts a person but God, the true judge of all.
He alone determines where favor rests.

PSALM 75:6, TPT

I name this day PROMOTION. It comes from You, God. Your eyes search to and fro, looking to show Yourself strong on behalf of those whose hearts are turned toward You.

Even if I lose it all, in You I have everything. You exalts me in due season. When I excel at my work, You promised that I would stand before kings. You grant me favor. You are the source of my PROMOTION.

That which requires manipulation to gain will also require manipulation to maintain. Promotion from God's hand, however, is secure. Turn your heart toward Him and His favor will overshadow you. Give yourself over to His timing today. Trust that He will promote you at the proper time.

HUMILITY

Do nothing out of selfish ambition or vain conceit.
Rather, in humility value others above yourselves,
not looking to your own interests but each
of you to the interests of the others.

PHILIPPIANS 2:3-4, NIV

I name this day HUMILITY. In honor, I will prefer others above myself. I will make sure that those I encounter are seen, heard, and valued.

I will measure opinions against love, keeping the big picture in mind. I will speak in kindness, truth wrapped in love, words clothed in HUMILITY.

Our culture rewards witty sarcasm, dark humor, calling attention to gaffes, and making fun of flaws. We polarize around opinions and thus, lose the opportunity to demonstrate love. Today, remember you have the mind of Christ. Let your speech be seasoned with grace, and walk in humility.

COVENANT

He always stands by His covenant—
the commitment He made to a thousand generations.

PSALM 105:8, NLT

I name this day COVENANT. I am Your child, a member of the royal priesthood, part of a holy nation. I love You with my whole heart, soul, mind, and strength. I also love my neighbor as myself.

You are faithful. You keep Your covenant for a thousand generations! As I love You and love people, I embrace all the blessings and promises that come from walking in Your COVENANT.

COVENANT: God's New Covenant with us
is unconditional—not sustained by our
performance because Jesus held up our end
of the bargain for us. God keeps His covenant
because of His worthiness, not ours.

As children of the covenant, we are the recipients of amazing promises. For more on the New Covenant, meditate on Jeremiah 31:31-34, Mark, 14:24, Luke 22:19-20, John 3:16, John 14:6, 1 Corinthians 11:25, 2 Corinthians 3:6, Hebrews 8:6-8, and Hebrews 9:15.

TOGETHER

In the human body there are many parts and organs, each with a unique function. And so it is in the body of Christ. For though we are many, we've all been mingled into one body in Christ. This means that we are all vitally joined to one another, with each contributing to the others.

ROMANS 12:4-5, TPT

I name this day TOGETHER. Life is better together. Our uniqueness is best expressed in the unity of the body of Christ. We are joined to each other meaningfully by God's design.

Sorrow, laughter, sadness, joy, burdens, blessings, revelation, questions ... these are all better when experienced TOGETHER.

The phrase "doing life together" is almost cliché in Christian circles. It is a glorious concept not often walked out meaningfully. But our hearts yearn for it nevertheless. We were born for vibrant community. Who do you "do life" with? Is this an area where you desire deeper connection?

RUNNING OVER

*Give, and you will receive. Your gift will return to you in
full—pressed down, shaken together to make room for
more, running over, and poured into your lap. The amount
you give will determine the amount you get back.*

LUKE 6:38, NLT

I name this day RUNNING OVER. To be found faithful in giving
requires that one also has the grace to receive. Good measure,
pressed down, shaken together, receive the RUNNING OVER!

---

*Do you struggle with giving? How about receiving? There are two sides
to this equation, and God's plan encompasses both. We are to give
freely and receive just as freely. If you struggle with either of these, stop
and ask why. Ponder your history and allow God to reveal Himself to
you in a greater measure through this kingdom principle.*

CONFIDENT HOPE

That hope is real and true, an anchor to steady our restless souls, a hope that leads us back behind the curtain to where God is (as the high priests did in the days when reconciliation flowed from sacrifices in the temple).

HEBREWS 6:19, VOICE

I name this day CONFIDENT HOPE. I trust in You, eternal God, and yield to sovereignty I cannot comprehend. You fill me with joy. When I allow myself to believe, I find peace.

Your hope is an anchor to my soul. It holds me when life's seas are troubled, and my soul grows restless. The reality of eternal restoration brings my soul hope I cannot begin to understand. By the power of Your Holy Spirit, I abound in CONFIDENT HOPE.

God's hope is indescribable. It is both an anchor and a life jacket. It tethers our heart to His promises and keeps us from floundering. Do you need hope today? Reach out to God and He will give you enough hope to satisfy your soul with enough left over to share.

AWARE

He has shown you, O mortal, what is good.
And what does the Lord require of you?
To act justly and to love mercy
and to walk humbly with your God.

MICAH 6:8, NIV

I name this day AWARE. I will keep my eyes open and pay attention. I will hold myself accountable for my actions and attitudes. I will seek to act justly, to love mercy, and to walk humbly with God. For me to see, hear, and value others, I must be AWARE.

AWARE: to possess knowledge or perceive
how your actions, thoughts, or emotions
align with your internal standards.

Self-awareness should lead to God-awareness. God-awareness should lead to self-awareness. Walking with God should take us on a never ending journey of personal growth and development. In what ways are you cultivating your self-awareness and personal growth?

STRENGTH OF MY HEART

My health may fail,
and my spirit may grow weak,
but God remains the strength of my heart;
He is mine forever.

PSALM 73:26, NLT

I name this day STRENGTH OF MY HEART. It comes from the joy of the Lord. The joy of the Lord is my strength. In the presence of the Lord, my joy becomes full.

It is not dependent on my health, my finances, my career, or any external situation. God's joy is the STRENGTH OF MY HEART.

Oh that you would live in God's joy! This is His heart for you. He desires that your joy would be made full, that you would experience His joy in complete measure. Let Him be the strength of your heart today. Get into His presence until you taste His joy.

AWE

*Let all the earth fear the Lord: let all the
inhabitants of the world stand in awe of Him.*

PSALM 33:8, KJV

I name this day AWE. May I open myself up to the God of wonders!
In a world bathed in special effects and unparalleled novelty, let
me approach the kingdom as a small child. Let each act of God be
a fresh miracle which inspires in me, AWE.

*AWE: a feeling of reverential respect mixed
with fear or wonder.*

*He is the God of miracles! His supernatural power is still active in the
earth today. It is easy to become jaded because of the faithlessness of
men, but cynicism is toxic to faith. Approach God with awe today and
let Him stir the miraculous in your soul.*

GOD SMILES

God bless you and keep you,
God smile on you and gift you,
God look you full in the face
and make you prosper.

NUMBERS 6:24-26, MSG

I name this day GOD SMILES. There is nothing that quite compares to standing in God's favor. Pray this prayer today: "God, bless and keep me. Smile on me, and let Your gaze of favor rest upon me. As You look me full in the face, I won't turn away. Give me peace and be gracious to me. Cause me to prosper. Put Your name on my children, mark them as Your own and bless them. Amen."

Claim God's promises. Bask in them. Let them wrap you in joy and uphold you in peace. Today, as you go about your routine, know that God is watching you—He has fixed His gaze upon you. He is with you. Know that GOD SMILES.

Take in a deep breath. Let it out slowly and smile up toward heaven. Smile at God and feel Him smile back at you. Step into the light of His countenance and behold Him in all His glory. The Lord is with you! He will give you peace and cause you to prosper. Amen.

SUPPLY

*But my God shall supply all your need according
to His riches in glory by Christ Jesus.*

PHILIPPIANS 4:19, KJV

I name this day SUPPLY. God, in You I have no lack; only access to abundance. I am not an orphan begging for bread. I do not need to toil for crumbs from Your table.

I am Yours. Therefore, a full measure of grace, joy, love, peace, hope, courage, and strength are available to me in rich SUPPLY.

What do you have need of today? What is in short supply for you at this very moment? Ask Him. He has promised to supply ALL your needs. The richness of His glory is yours for the partaking. Today, step into God's supernatural supply!

FOREVER

The grass withers and the flowers fall,
but the word of our God endures forever.

ISAIAH 40:8, NIV

I name this day FOREVER. That's the perspective I want to keep in mind. What is momentary, what is temporal, what is eternal? Each has their purpose and deserves appropriate attention. Only one, however, is worthy to serve as a plumbline. Today, may everything that screams for my attention be measured against that which lasts FOREVER.

When we neglect what is important long enough, we find ourselves in crisis. Unfulfilled and enduring consequences. Look at your schedule today. What is momentary? What is temporal? What is eternal? Does your time investment reflect these priorities? If not, what can you adjust to address that which is of greatest importance?

NOVEMBER

O give thanks unto the Lord;
for He is good;
for His mercy endureth for ever.

1 CHRONICLES 16:34, KJV

CHOSEN

*Before I even formed you in your mother's womb,
I knew all about you. Before you drew your
first breath, I had already chosen you
to be My prophet to speak My word to the nations.*

JEREMIAH 1:5, VOICE

I name this day CHOSEN. Before I was even formed, You chose me. Before I drew my first breath, You had appointed me—filled me with purpose, designed my personality, blended my gifts, and established me as Your child.

I am Yours. When I want to compare my gifts to others or criticize how I look or what I can do, I will remember that it was You who fashioned me. Your design. I am peculiar—special and particular. I have been set apart. I am CHOSEN.

Ponder what it means to be chosen by God. This is incredible! You have been set apart for His service. What does it mean to you to be part of the royal priesthood? How does it make you feel to be chosen by God?

NOVEMBER 2

HOLD STEADY

*We have this hope as an anchor for
the soul, firm and secure.*

HEBREWS 6:19a, NIV

I name this day HOLD STEADY. In seasons of uncertainty, I hold to truth so I won't get crushed by facts. Facts change. Truth remains.

I decree solid footing today. I hold fast to the promises of God. I cling to the Rock. Through every storm, He is the anchor that causes me to HOLD STEADY.

God is your fortress. He is the Solid Rock. When things around you are uncertain or you feel challenged by circumstances, put your hope in God. This hope is an anchor for your soul. What facts in your life need to be confronted with God's truth?

HIDDEN

For in the day of trouble
He will keep me safe in His dwelling;
He will hide me in the shelter of His sacred tent
and set me high upon a rock.

PSALM 27:5, NIV

I name this day HIDDEN. I am under the shadow of Your wing. I am covered and sheltered in Your tabernacle. There I am safe.

Today I decree You are my shield. You are my fortress and strong tower. You set me high upon a rock. No harm shall come near me. Though a host may encamp and surround me, power belongs to God! In You, I am HIDDEN.

What a comfort to know that you are hidden by God. He camouflages you from your enemies. He sets you high on a rock—gives you the high ground where you can see them coming from the safety of His dwelling place. Be still today and rest in the safety that comes from being hidden with Christ in God.

MERRY HEART

A merry heart doeth good like a medicine:
but a broken spirit drieth the bones.

PROVERBS 17:22, KJV

I name this day MERRY HEART—

It is good like medicine, and salve for the soul.

It is light dispersing shadow; happy, well, and whole.

When on good things my heart does dwell,

My mouth fills with praise, and my joy will swell.

When cheerful is my countenance, and laughter does abound,

then hope springs forth with gladness, and it blesses all around.

I shall this day give praise to God from the very start;

I am thankful He has given me a very MERRY HEART!

Laughter is good medicine. Science has proved this out. Laughter releases endorphines, quiets pain receptors, and gives people a more positive outlook which helps their brains engage with healing. Is your heart merry? What will it take to let your heart be glad and rejoice?

INVENTIVE IN HOSPITALITY

Don't burn out; keep yourselves fueled and aflame.
Be alert servants of the Master, cheerfully expectant.
Don't quit in hard times; pray all the harder.
Help needy Christians; be inventive in hospitality.

ROMANS 12:11-13, MSG

I name this day INVENTIVE IN HOSPITALITY. I see the connection between "fueled and aflame" and meaningful community. Therefore, I open my life—my heart and my home. When I share my story authentically, that is a place to start. When I invite people into shared experience, it becomes a place to stay. This fueling of each other's spirits results from being INVENTIVE IN HOSPITALITY.

The early church was known for breaking bread together and going from house to house. What does the phrase "inventive in hospitality" mean to you? In what ways can you practice inventive hospitality to keep yourself fueled and aflame for God?

MOTION

Put your heart and soul into every activity
you do, as though you are doing it for the
Lord himself and not merely for others.

COLOSSIANS 3:23, TPT

I name this day MOTION. I am consistently moving in the direction where I am aimed. I commit my work to the Lord.

Today my plans take me closer to my goals. Today I acknowledge my direction and make adjustments to my course, allowing the Lord to establish my steps. God, make my aim true. I am growing. I am changing. I am in forward MOTION.

Newton's First Law parallels a spiritual law. When we are at rest, we tend to remain at rest. When we are in motion, we tend to remain in motion. Motion provides momentum and overcomes spiritual inertia. Are you stuck or in motion?

SAFE

God is a safe place to hide,
ready to help when we need Him.
We stand fearless at the cliff-edge of doom,
courageous in seastorm and earthquake,
before the rush and roar of oceans, the tremors
that shift mountains. Jacob-wrestling God fights
for us, God-of-Angel-Armies protects us.

PSALM 46:1-3, MSG

I name this day SAFE. Under the shadow of Your wing, I hide. I have courage because I know You are with me, before and behind. What I fear is no match for Your love and mighty power. Troubles, even of my own making, melt in Your presence.

I am fearless and courageous because you fight for me. Because You protect me, I am SAFE.

Imagine a small child, alone in the dark, answering a suspicious knock. Now imagine that same child wrapped in her Father's arms in the full light of day, her companion as Father answers the door. His authority protects. Her security is in His power and ability to handle whatever comes. You are the child. Drink in the safety of His arms around you.

TENACITY

*Our suffering is light and temporary and
is producing for us an eternal glory that is
greater than anything we can imagine.*

2 CORINTHIANS 4:17, GW

I name this day TENACITY. I will hold to my course, eyes on the prize, knowing I will see the goodness of God. I will not lose heart when momentary, light affliction threatens my hope.

I won't get stuck worrying about things that are temporary. Instead, I will look upon His face and persevere with TENACITY.

*TENACITY: the quality of being persistent,
determined, holding fast.*

Are you going through a trial? Paul describes our suffering as light and temporary and encourages us that enduring the trial produces in us an eternal glory. Hold fast. Ask God to give you an eternal perspective that helps you put difficult things into perspective.

NOVEMBER 9

INSIGHT

*Carefully consider all that I've taught you, and
may our Lord inspire you with wisdom and
revelation in everything you say and do.*

2 TIMOTHY 2:7, TPT

I name this day INSIGHT. Let me be open to hear instruction, receive revelation, and activate adjustment. Illuminate me, Lord with light from Your Word, and from it may I find fresh INSIGHT.

*INSIGHT: the capacity to gain an accurate and
deep intuitive understanding.*

Open your heart to hear and receive instruction. Meditate on God's Word, read other books, and listen to wisdom and counsel from trusted sources. Ask God to grant you wisdom and revelation. His insight will guide you in everything you say and do. It will give you an edge, and help you navigate every relationship.

NOVEMBER 10

FITLY SPOKEN

Let the words of my mouth and the meditation
of my heart be acceptable in Your sight,
O Lord, my strength and my Redeemer.

PSALM 91:11, NIV

A word fitly spoken is like apples of gold
in a setting of silver.

PROVERBS 25:11, ESV

I name this day FITLY SPOKEN. Let the words of my mouth and the meditation of my heart be acceptable in Your sight. May my speech be seasoned with grace, like an apple of gold set in pure silver. May life, peace, healing, and strength flow through me as I utter words FITLY SPOKEN.

Your words shape your world. The tone as well as the word choice creates an atmosphere of blessing or curse, positivity and possibility, or negativity and calamity. The choice is yours. Pay attention to your words today. Let them be as apples of gold in settings of silver. May your words be fitly spoken.

LOYAL

A friend is always loyal, and a brother
is born to help in time of need.

PROVERBS 17:17, NLT

I name this day LOYAL. I stand with friends and family in good times and bad. Whether fine dining or in fox holes, I'm there.

I am a good friend. I am a faithful companion. I count myself rich because of those in my life who are LOYAL.

Who are your friends? Take a few minutes to consider who is with you through thick and thin, who you could call upon and who knows they could call on you and you would answer. Speak their names out loud and offer a prayer of thanskgiving for them. Reach out today and let them know they were on your mind.

POURED OUT

As you go, proclaim this message: "The kingdom of heaven has come near." Heal the sick, raise the dead, cleanse those who have leprosy, drive out demons. Freely you have received; freely give.

MATTHEW 10:7-8, NIV

I name this day POURED OUT. Father, as you fill me I will faithfully pour into others. Everything I am is from You. Everything I understand is through You.

I will proclaim that the kingdom of heaven is near. Give me the faith to heal the sick, raise the dead, cleanse those with disease, and drive out demons. Freely You have given to me, so freely I give to others. May I remember always from whence I came and live a life POURED OUT.

Gratitude and generosity go hand in hand. When you realize that absolutely everything you possess comes from God, you can become a conduit for it to flow through rather than a container for it to collect. In what ways can you pour yourself out to others today?

RESILIENT

Yet even in the midst of all these things,
we triumph over them all, for God has made us to
be more than conquerors, and His demonstrated
love is our glorious victory over everything!

ROMANS 8:37, TPT

I name this day RESILIENT. I bounce back. I persevere. I endure. Endurance causes me to grow. I will not allow failure to stick to me. My plans are submitted to the Lord and they succeed. I submit to godly counsel and learn from mistakes as well as from a job well executed.

I do not just survive, I thrive. I am more than a conqueror, and I have the victory. I am RESILIENT.

RESILIENT: able to spring back into shape after
bending, able to withstand and recover quickly
from difficult situations.

You are stronger than you think. Your ability to endure difficult situations is amazing. You are more than a conqueror. You are victorious. Your resilience is testimony to God's character at work in your life. Pause and thank God for causing you to triumph.

SOUND MIND

For God has not given us the spirit of fear;
but of power and of love and of a sound mind.

2 TIMOTHY 1:7, NKJV

I name this day SOUND MIND. Because God has given me the spirit of love and the spirit of power, He removes the spirit of fear from the equation.

I have the mind of Christ, and I can access the resources of heaven. I take my thoughts captive. I meditate on good things. I speak words of life and release the Word of God over my thoughtful, positive, hopeful, SOUND MIND.

There are many studies out there to prove that we can literally re-wire our brains. The damage done by toxic, limiting, fearful thoughts can be reversed by intentionally replacing them with hopeful, positive, peace-filled ones. How is the state of your mind?

FAVOR

My child, never forget the things I have taught you.
Store my commands in your heart. If you do this, you
will live many years, and your life will be satisfying.
Never let loyalty and kindness leave you! Tie them around
your neck as a reminder. Write them deep within your heart.
Then you will find favor with both God and people,
and you will earn a good reputation.

PROVERBS 3:1-4, NLT

I name this day FAVOR. God's affection towards me attracts heaven's resources to me, so He can work through me!

There is favor on my assignment, therefore God's hand of blessing is with me whether I am high or low. In all things He is at work for my good. In all seasons, my soul can prosper. I step into agreement with God and gratefully embrace His FAVOR.

The favor of God is a beautiful thing. It can cause even your adversaries to agree with you and help you. Step into God's favor today. Open yourself to receive it as His gift. Position yourself for it by walking in obedience. Let the favor of God go before you!

WHAT GOD BUILDS

For we are co-workers in God's service;
you are God's field, God's building.

1 CORINTHIANS 3:9, NIV

I name this day WHAT GOD BUILDS. I delight to be a co-worker in God's field. I want to put my hands to what He is building lest my work be in vain. But what God builds remains.

Gold, silver, and costly stones are materials that last. Wood, hay, and straw will not stand the test of fire. I want to be a wise builder who works with care, building upon a firm foundation of WHAT GOD BUILDS.

My mentor often says, "God is not obligated to bless what He does not build." That sticks with me. Whenever I begin or join a project, I ask God if He is building this house or if I am running off on my own. I want my work to be blessed. I want to build things which will remain. What do you sense God is building in your life? How can you co-labor with Him?

SATISFIED

Let them praise the Lord for His great love
and for the wonderful things He has done for them.
For He satisfies the thirsty
and fills the hungry with good things.

PSALM 107:8-9, NLT

I name this day SATISFIED. Your love, O Lord, is great, and I am amazed at all the wonderful things You have done. You satisfy the longing in my soul. You answer my hungry soul by filling it with good things.

When my soul prospers, everything else prospers. Teach me to nurture my soul. I embrace Your sufficiency today, and I am blissfully SATISFIED.

SATISFIED: pleased, content with what has been
received, paid in full, persuaded by evidence.

How is your soul? As Christians, we learn to feed our spirit man, but often mistakenly equate the soul with the flesh and are taught to deny it. That leads to a languishing soul, and when our soul does not prosper, we cannot prosper and be in good health (3 John 2). What would it look like for your soul to be satisfied?

REST

*By the seventh day God had finished the work He
had been doing. On the seventh day He stopped
the work He had been doing. Then God blessed the
seventh day and set it apart as holy, because on
that day He stopped all His work of creation.*

GENESIS 2:2-3, GW

I name this day REST. The Creator of the universe rested after He worked. Jesus pulled away and went off by Himself to rest after He ministered. God established the Sabbath as a gift for us. He demonstrated for us how to establish a healthy rhythm of work and rest.

God, I struggle to unplug from responsibilities and tasks and to-do lists. Even when I sit down, my mind keeps running. When I am weary, my joy drains away. When I am tired, it is hard to dream or pursue my purpose with passion. Teach me to rest. Help me re-wire my brain that rest is not lazy but a strategy. The only way to live as a wise steward is to understand, embrace, and implement the principle of REST.

Do you struggle with being over-busy? Do you feel guilty if you take time to pause and let your body and your mind enjoy a respite? It is easy to become a slave to our schedule. Survey it today. Check in with your body. Is it tired? How about your emotions? Are they weary? Take care of yourself. Carve out time to rest. Rhythmically rest.

EVERY VALLEY EXALTED

*The voice of one crying in the wilderness: "Prepare the
way of the Lord; make straight in the desert a highway
for our God. Every valley shall be exalted and every
mountain and hill brought low; the crooked places shall
be made straight and the rough places smooth; the
glory of the Lord shall be revealed, and all flesh shall see
it together; for the mouth of the Lord has spoken."*

ISAIAH 40:3-5, NKJV

I name this day EVERY VALLEY EXALTED. When I walk with God, trusting Him with the big picture and the timing, even my valleys become higher ground.

God, you make my rough places smooth, you straighten out what is crooked, you bring my obstacles low. When I am patient and engage the process, Your glory is revealed in me. Today I stand on this truth, and I know in due season I will see EVERY VALLEY EXALTED.

We go from glory to glory. In between each of those glories, there is transition. Those transition journeys are full of valleys and mountains, rough roads, crooked paths, stones, sand traps ... you name it! But God. God walks with you through each transition. He makes the rough places smooth and with Him, even your valleys are higher ground!

PREPARED PLACE

And if I go and prepare a place for you,
I will come again and receive you to Myself;
that where I am, there you may be also.

JOHN 14:3, NKJV

I name this day PREPARED PLACE. Preparation is an act of honor. It is the anticipation of joyful connection which leads to the willing sacrifice of things "now" to make reverent room for things "next."

Father, I awaken to the love behind Your preparation of a place for me. Now in my heart and through my actions, my joy at being received is kindled. I want to be with You. I make my heart ready and my spirit soars as I step into Your PREPARED PLACE.

God has prepared a place for you. It isn't a last minute scurry, you didn't take Him by surprise. He knew you were coming—He knew you would receive Him! And He has utilized eternity to prepare a place where you will come and dine with Him, where you will sit in His presence and fellowship with Him. How does this make you feel?

PROCLAIM JUSTICE

Say no to wrong.
Learn to do good.
Work for justice.
Help the down-and-out.
Stand up for the homeless.
Go to bat for the defenseless.

ISAIAH 1:17, MSG

I name this day PROCLAIM JUSTICE. God lives in me, I am His child. Mercy and justice are my inherited garments. I survey my surroundings in the clear light of day. I will not turn a blind eye, I will not wink at injustice, I will not pretend it isn't there. I won't keep silent for the sake of my security or comfort or reputation. No, I see and I speak up for the voiceless. As heaven's ambassador I PROCLAIM JUSTICE.

Look around. What captures your notice? Ask God to highlight to you what (and who) is not being treated justly. It is easy to put our heads in the sand and pretend it is someone else's problem, but if we look away and say nothing, we are part of the problem. Ask God to give you His heart of justice, that what breaks His heart will also break yours.

NOT DISMAYED

"So don't be afraid. I am here, with you;
don't be dismayed, for I am your God.
I will strengthen you, help you.
I am here with My right hand to
make right and to hold you up."

ISAIAH 41:10, VOICE

I name this day NOT DISMAYED. When the speed of life is too fast, when things beyond my control spin 'round about me, when frustrations arise, I am grateful, God, that You are near. You are my God who never leaves. You strengthen me. You help me. You uphold me with Your righteous right hand. I will not fear. I am NOT DISMAYED.

DISMAYED: loss of courage or resolution
because of alarm or fear.

Isaiah's words are strong encouragement to us. God is with us. Regardless of the news cycle, any threat to our finances or health or family—be not dismayed. God will strenthen and help you. He has promised to hold you up. Take courage. Remain resolved. God's got you!

ONLY ONE

And the Lord will be King over all the earth;
on that day the Lord will be the only
one, and His name the only one.

ZECHARIAH 14:9, NASB

I name this day ONLY ONE. God, You are sovereign and You reign over land, sea, and sky. You are King over all the earth, King over my life. What an honor to be in service to the All-Powerful, All-Seeing, All-Knowing One who reigns over all. You alone are God, and Your name is above every other name. It is the ONLY ONE.

As a child we read stories of knights and ladies and noble deeds in service to their king. There is a reason this resonates with us. Our hearts quicken to tales of honor, duty, and fealty. We serve the King of kings! We serve the Lord of lords! Suit up in your spiritual armor today and boldy display the colors. God your King receives your service as worship!

HE GIVES

*He gives power to the weak, and to those who
have no might He increases strength.*

ISAIAH 40:29, NKJV

I name this day HE GIVES. Sometimes when I am confident and strong, when things are breaking my way, it is easy to believe I'm the driving force behind my good times. Funny how when it all goes south, I quickly run back to God for protection, comfort, and help.

Today, I choose to remember the Source of my supply—whatever season I'm in. I am grateful I am never alone and that from His inexhaustible resources, HE GIVES.

God gives power to the weak. He increases strength to those who have no might. He owns the cattle on a thousand hills. The earth and all it contains is His. The universe is His to command. Whatever you have need of, He has an immeasurable supply. Ask. Come boldly before His throne and ask. He is the God who gives.

VALUE

Sweet friendships refresh the soul and
awaken our hearts with joy,
for good friends are like the anointing oil
that yields the fragrant incense of God's presence.

PROVERBS 27:9, TPT

I name this day VALUE. As I survey the people in my life, I am filled with gratitude.

Today I will reach out to those God brings to my mind and express to them their worth. I will be faithful to encourage them. I will tell them I care and let them know what they mean to me. I am rich beyond measure, my life is filled with people of extreme VALUE.

Ask God to highlight someone to you today, and reach out to them. A call or text, a handwritten note or a gift. Respond in obedience to encourage and build up whoever God brings to your mind. Allow the Holy Spirit to use you today to demonstrate love and communicate their value.

SENT OUT

Again Jesus said, "Peace be with you!
As the Father has sent Me,
I am sending you."

JOHN 20:21, NIV

I name this day SENT OUT. Light. Salt. Bringer of hope. Kingdom operative. Servant. Treasure hunter. Joy bell. In the world but not of it. Mighty in spirit. Excelling at my work. Standing out as one branded by Love. Wise. Kind. Clever. Winning at life. This is how I show up when I tap into what heaven has placed in my heart, and I remember I am one who has been SENT OUT.

You are not your own, you have been bought with a price. You are an ambassador of heaven. A child of God. The bride of Christ. The servant of all. You have been given all authority in heaven and empowered to perform the Great Commission. You are sent out. How will you show up in that role today?

SEE AND TREMBLE

His lightnings light the world; the earth sees and trembles.
The mountains melt like wax at the presence of the Lord,
At the presence of the Lord of the whole earth.

PSALM 97:4-6, NKJV

I name this day SEE and TREMBLE. The heavens declare the glory of God. All creation resounds with praise. Nature knows. Where she is wild, untamed by man, unbridled in how she sprawls and expands and worships the Creator, you can literally feel the glory of God. You can sense the memory imprint of the Garden. There in the stillness, with awe and wonder my only vocabulary, I SEE AND TREMBLE.

The next time a storm is brewing, find a spot where you can watch it roll in and appreciate the beauty and majesty of the lightning and thunder. Stand at the shore and watch waves crash on the rocks. The whole earth trembles at God's presence and it testifies of His greatness. What a thing to witness!

ONE VOICE

May God, who gives this patience and encouragement,
help you live in complete harmony with each other, as
is fitting for followers of Christ Jesus. Then all of you
can join together with one voice, giving praise and
glory to God, the Father of our Lord Jesus Christ.

ROMANS 15:5-6, NLT

I name this day ONE VOICE. My heart longs for unity. My soul sings when I am surrounded by the resonance of like-minded hearts in one accord. There is nothing quite like the joy of being a synchronous part of a glorious, unified whole! Today, may I find members of my tribe, so together we can glorify God, the Father, with the power and beauty of ONE VOICE.

There is nothing quite like connecting with those of like nature and ability. The fellowship of the saints builds us up. In isolation, we are more easily distracted and discouraged. Whatever your fellowship situation, as much as possible, seek out opportunities to connect with others in corporate worship. The unity of one voice brings power!

GIVE STABILITY

A leader of good judgment gives stability;
an exploiting leader leaves a trail of waste.

PROVERBS 29:4, MSG

I name this day GIVE STABILITY. When I lead well, those in my charge feel safe, they are informed, and they have what they need to succeed so they can thrive in their abilities.

No trail of waste behind me, I leave pathways of light, hope, and glory. I embrace the strength of God in me and by His grace, I GIVE STABILITY.

What kind of leader do you like to follow? What kind of leader do you purpose to be? You lead someone. Who is in your circle of influence that your character and conduct make a difference? Decide today to be a leader who gives stability. Develop your leadership skills with intention.

HONOR GOD

*Whether you eat or drink, live your life in a
way that glorifies and honors God.*

1 CORINTHIANS 10:31, TPT

I name this day HONOR GOD. When I start the day filled with gratitude, and I count my blessings while resting in hope, I step into the wonder of God's sovereignty. I delight in being cared for, loved, and protected. In the sweetness of this citizenship, I am free.

When I meditate on God's goodness and seek to build His character into my own; when I endeavor to see people through His eyes and love them as He does; when I speak and act and live my life in a way the glorifies Him, I HONOR GOD.

*HONOR: regard with great respect, show great
esteem, adhere to a standard of right conduct.*

What does it mean to you to live your life in a way that honors God? Let it be love that compels you, not the law. Let the joy of His presence quicken you to walk worthy of His calling. What does honor look like for you?

DECEMBER

For unto us a Child is born,
unto us a Son is given:
and the government shall be upon His shoulder:
and His name shall be called
Wonderful,
Counselor,
The Mighty God,
The Everlasting Father,
The Prince of Peace.

ISAIAH 9:6, KJV

COME WITH ME

I hear the Lord saying, "I will stay close to you,
instructing and guiding you along the pathway for your life.
I will advise you along the way
and lead you forth with My eyes as your guide.
So don't make it difficult; don't be stubborn
when I take you where you've not been before.
Don't make me tug you and pull you along.
Just come with me!"

PSALM 32:8, TPT

I name this day COME WITH ME. Change is first sparked in the heart, then confirmed in the mind. Change moves from the mind to the mouth where the decree is made, repeated, and rehearsed.

Finally, with agreement between heart, head, and mouth, change at last is activated and can begin to bear fruit. God, I won't be stubborn when You take me down new and unfamiliar paths. I open myself up for change. I will answer Your call to "COME WITH ME."

Growth without change is impossible. Change without uncertainty is a myth. Change is rarely comfortable. But God wants to take you down paths you have not before been on. He has new territory for you to occupy, new adventures for your heart to taste. When He says, "Come with Me," what will you answer?

COME TO MY LIGHT

Nations shall come to Your light,
and kings to the brightness of Your rising.

ISAIAH 60:3, NKJV

I name this day COME TO MY LIGHT. I will arise and shine. I am radiant with joy. I am bright with love. My lamp shines out hope. I am a beacon of encouragement and kindness. At the brightness of my rising, people COME TO MY LIGHT!

Arise, shine, for the glory of the Lord is risen upon you! You are a city set on a hill whose light cannot be hidden. Light pours forth from your spirit everywhere you go, challenging darkness, exposing evil, radiating warmth and comfort. How is the brightness of your light?

EVERLASTING STRENGTH

If you fail under pressure, your strength is too small.

PROVERBS 24:10, NLT

Trust ye in the Lord forever: for in the
Lord Jehovah is everlasting strength.

ISAIAH 26:4, KJV

I name this day EVERLASTING STRENGTH. My strength endures by constant renewal and replenishment by God's joy. I will not fail in times of adversity. Each time I stand before the throne in God's presence, I am energized and recharged with EVERLASTING STRENGTH.

In the presence of the Lord, there is fullness of joy, and the joy of the Lord is your strength. God, the Lord Jehovah, is everlasting strength, and He has promised you access to His never-ending supply. You will not falter under pressure. Your strength will not fail in adversity. God, your God, will strengthen you.

BELIEVE AND RECEIVE

Therefore, I tell you, whatever you ask for in prayer,
believe that you have received it, and it will be yours.

MARK 11:24, NIV

I name this day BELIEVE AND RECEIVE. Father, here is my faith, planted in the soil of hope. Cause it to grow. Help my unbelief.

Kindle fires of expectancy and guide my desires until my prayers align with Your will. With childlike wonder, I will ask in prayer. In faith, I BELIEVE AND RECEIVE.

Even when we struggle with belief, God has made provision for us. He told us we could pray, "Help my unbelief." What is it that you need to receive today? Are you struggling to believe that God will answer—not that He can, but that He will? Breathe the prayer, "Help my unbelief," then position yourself to believe and receive today.

DO WHAT HE TELLS YOU

But regarding anything beyond this, dear friend,
go easy. There's no end to the publishing of books,
and constant study wears you out so you're no
good for anything else. The last and final word
is this: Fear God. Do what He tells you.

ECCLESIASTES 12:12-13, MSG

I name this day DO WHAT HE TELLS YOU. Life can be too much toil, too much struggle, too much wondering if you are headed the right way, too much concern over how tomorrow will unfold. Work, work, work; try, try, try. But such comfort surrounds us when we lay down striving and embrace the simpler path to just DO WHAT HE TELLS YOU.

When Jesus performed His first miracle at Cana, His mother looked at the servants (I imagine with a twinkle in her eye), and said, "Do whatever He tells you" (John 2:5). Obedience is required to live a victorious life. Obedience is a blessing because we don't have to do things on our own. What is God telling you to do?

DECEMBER 6

HEAD IN THE GAME

*So roll up your sleeves,
get your head in the game,
be totally ready to receive the gift that's
coming when Jesus arrives.*

1 PETER 1:14, MSG

I name this day HEAD IN THE GAME. I heighten my self-awareness. I increase my others-awareness. Most importantly, I tune into my God-awareness. I will use the gifts God gave me in ways that bring honor to His name.

I roll up my sleeves, shake off my sleepy-headed, foggy-brained, in-a-daze thinking and put my HEAD IN THE GAME.

The world needs what you've got! God desires for you to partner with Him to bring the kingdom of heaven to earth. This doesn't happen by accident. You aren't a silent partner, you are an active, creative participant in the unfolding will of the Father. Make sure you have your head—and heart—in the game!

GIVE WAY TO LAUGHTER

All you saints! Sing your hearts out to God!
Thank Him to His face!
He gets angry once in a while,
but across a lifetime there is only love.
The nights of crying your eyes out
give way to days of laughter.

PSALM 30:4-5 MSG

I name this day GIVE WAY TO LAUGHTER. Weeping endures for a night, and sometimes that night is very long and very dark indeed. But night gives way to morning, and with the new day joy cometh.

The return of joy added to sustained hope is something incredible to experience. In that tension of expectation, when tears are still fresh on your cheeks, be restored as you GIVE WAY TO LAUGHTER.

Every storm runs out of rain, and yours will too. The cycle and circle of life brings tears and laughter. Each season accomplishes something that can only be accessed through that experience. God is love. He is a good Father, and He cares for you. He captures your tears in a bottle as a remembrance, and He laughs with joy when morning comes for you.

COUNSELOR

God-lovers make the best counselors.
Their words possess wisdom and are right and trustworthy.
The ways of God are in their hearts, and they won't
swerve from the paths of steadfast righteousness.

PSALM 37:30-31, TPT

I name this day COUNSELOR. Because I am a lover of God, my words are wise and trustworthy. God's ways are dear to me; they are in my heart, part of me, so I do not swerve from a righteous path even when life squeezes me. What I have learned, I gladly share. I care deeply about others and I am honored to serve as a dependable guide and faithful COUNSELOR.

You always have access to The Counselor. He lives in you. Whenever you feel at a loss for words or are unsure how to offer comfort or guidance, you can connect to the Holy Spirit and let His love and wisdom flow through you. When God's ways are in your heart, you cannot help but be a faithful counselor.

EXCEEDINGLY ABUNDANT

*Now unto Him that is able to do exceeding
abundantly above all that we ask or think,
according to the power that worketh in us,
unto Him be glory in the church by Christ Jesus
throughout all ages, world without end. Amen.*

EPHESIANS 3:20-21, KJV

I name this day EXCEEDINGLY ABUNDANT. I walk in extravagant love. I live in a place of supernatural expectation. I marvel at the goodness of God. I am blown away by every facet of His creation.

How extravagant that He has adopted me into His family! How incomprehensible that He would give me His name, place me under His protection, and authorize me as royalty throughout His kingdom!

I see His handiwork everywhere. I hear Him when birds sing, when children laugh, and when thunder echoes. He who knows no sin became sin for me that I might forever live and move and have my being in Him. This is love EXCEEDINGLY ABUNDANT!

Step into the beauty and bounty of God's exceedingly abundant power, greatness, and love! Reach into the supernatural reality of God's exceedingly abundant nature. Open yourself up to experience Him in this way. Let Him show you this side of His personality—you won't be disappointed!

PRUDENCE

I, wisdom, dwell with prudence,
And find out knowledge and discretion.

PROVERBS 8:12, NKJV

I name this day PRUDENCE. Lord, help me to say the right things at the right times in the right places. Even more, help me to resist releasing the witty cutting remark on the tip of my tongue, the zinger when a perfect moment arises and temptation to deliver a well-deserved blow is high. Instead, season my speech with grace, help me to avoid creating blunders. I choose wisdom's friend as my companion. I welcome PRUDENCE.

PRUDENCE: the friend of wisdom, prudence
deliberates and consults the most suitable
means to accomplish valuable purposes, it
works to foresee and avoid evil and calamity.

Prudence is a word from a bygone era. You rarely hear it spoken. Yet, prudence is wisdom applied to practice. It allows us to discern and select our actions with appropriate caution, with the both the end and the means to that end in our view. In what ways can you develop the quality of prudence in your life?

SEIZE AND HOLD TIGHTLY

*Let us seize and hold tightly the confession of our
hope without wavering, for He who promised is
reliable and trust worthy and faithful [to His word].*

HEBREWS 10:23, AMP

I name this day SEIZE AND HOLD TIGHTLY. Mild, lightly held convictions do not keep me in a storm. Head knowledge which has not penetrated to my heart and taken anchor in the depths of my soul will not guide me when life's shifting sands and tempestuous seas challenge my core beliefs. What keeps my course steady is truth that I SEIZE and to which I HOLD TIGHTLY.

What are your convictions? Are you aware of and able to describe your theology? What you believe matters a great deal. When times of testing or trial come, what you believe will either hold you steady, or cause you to veer far off course. Is your "head knowledge" and "heart experience" in alignment? Spend some time articulating your beliefs.

ASSURANCE

*... and since we have a great priest over the house of
God, let us draw near with a true heart in full assurance
of faith, with our hearts sprinkled clean from an evil
conscience and our bodies washed with pure water.*

HEBREWS 3:21b-22, ESV

I name this day ASSURANCE. I will not fear the contradictions I experience or yield my hope for the future to the pain of my present. My heart is true, and I will draw near to God. My steps have been ordered by God. My path has purpose. He will perfect that which concerns me. In His unfailing love, I place my full, complete ASSURANCE.

*ASSURANCE: firm persuasion, full confidence or
trust, freedom from doubt,
the utmost certainty.*

You've heard the hymn, "Blessed assurance, Jesus is mine ..." Assurance is certainty. Websters 1828 Dictionary says "utmost certainty." The blood of Jesus shed for us grants us access to the holy place where God dwells. We have entered into this new and lasting covenant with Him. Stand on the full, firm assurance of this today.

BEAUTIFUL

You are beautiful in every way,
my true love.
There is no blemish on you.

SONG OF SONGS 4:7, GW

I name this day BEAUTIFUL. There is beauty to be found all around me. If I look for it, I will find it. Today I will look for the unexpected. I will look deeper than the surface and acknowledge the divine in the ordinary. I will set my awareness to notice that even in places where others do not see it, I will discover what is BEAUTIFUL.

Do you feel beautiful? When you look in the mirror, do you first notice blemishes, flaws, or things you think are unlovely? How about your insides? Do they feel beautiful, or is it easier to judge what we know still needs work? God looks at you through the blood of Jesus. He sees you as spotless and blemish free. When He looks at you, He sees only beauty. Drink that in.

SOUL HEALTH

*Beloved, I pray that you may prosper in all things
and be in health, just as your soul prospers.*

3 JOHN 2, NKJV

I name this day SOUL HEALTH. Today I will faithfully feed my soul. I will fill it with good things and nurture it well. When I ignore it, my bones wither, my spirit lacks, my heart grows weary. In order to prosper in all things, I must attend to my SOUL HEALTH.

What feeds your soul? Do you know? Is it nature? Books? Music? Time with friends? Solitude? Tending to the health of your soul goes beyond self-care. It is important to your spiritual, mental, emotional, and physical well being. Assess your soul's health. Make a plan to feed it what it needs so it can prosper.

CALLED TO SERVE

*You are to lead by a different model. If you want
to be the greatest, then live as one called to serve
others. The path to promotion comes by having the
heart of a bond-slave who serves everyone.*

MARK 10:43-44, TPT

I name this day CALLED TO SERVE. I will lead by a different model, God, the way Jesus did, as a servant of all. This takes grace. On my own it is easy to serve those I like and who seem deserving, but harder with those who are disagreeable, manipulative, or rude. I start out well-intentioned, then fade fast when I encounter that character. So, help me. Give me Your eyes. The ones that see the long-gone and take in the end from the beginning. The ones that saw how they were formed and fashioned before life twisted Your beauty into hardness and hate.

This is more than an idealistic "ought to," my heart is quickened to reach for a heaven-breathed "want to." So today, God, let the song of heaven stir in me so I will remember that I am CALLED TO SERVE.

Mark instructs us to live as one called to serve others, and he tells us that service is the path to promotion. Check your heart. Do you find it easy to lay down your life and serve, or does it rub you the wrong way or cause you to struggle or need recognition? A heart like Jesus is the heart of a servant.

GO FOR THE GOAL

*I leave the past behind and with hands outstretched
to whatever lies ahead I go straight for the goal—my
reward the honour of being called by God in Christ.*

PHILIPPIANS 3:14, PHILLIPS

I name this day GO FOR THE GOAL. I celebrate others who have run a leg of their race with purpose and intention and passed a milestone on the way to their goals.

Celebrating markers is important. Each marks progress to great goals. I will take the time to look back and say, "Job well done." This sets me up for the next leg of my journey. I will keep running hard. I will GO FOR THE GOAL.

Do you have clear goals? What has God called you to do? What dreams has He placed in your heart? Have you shared these dreams with someone you trust who can encourage you and hold you accountable to the goals along the way?

FIX MY GAZE

So, we don't look at the troubles we can see now;
rather, we fix our gaze on things that cannot be seen.

2 CORINTHIANS 4:18, NLT

I name this day FIX MY GAZE. The things which fight for my focus distract me from the prize. These things can compromise my joy, threaten my security, and confuse my plans. But I have an alternative. I have the great privilege of touching heaven's perspective and gaining the vantage point of the Spirit. So, it is upon these unseen things I choose to FIX MY GAZE.

Hold up your hand and look at it. Notice how the background fades away. Now, look at the horizon. Notice how your hand fades from view. Where does your focus lie? What holds your gaze? Choose heaven's perspective today.

MEMORIALS

... and take up each of you a stone upon his shoulder,
... that this may be a sign among you. When your children
ask in time to come, "What do those stones mean to you?"
then you shall tell them the waters of the Jordan were cut
off before the ark of the covenant of the Lord. ... So these
stones shall be to the people of Israel a memorial forever.

JOSHUA 4:5b-7, ESV

I name this day MEMORIALS. Thank you, God, for giving me markers in my journey. They help me measure my progress and remember Your faithfulness to me. I will reflect on what You have done and on what I have learned. I will use this knowledge to guide my efforts for the coming season.

I will pause and give thanks. I will build an altar to you in my heart. I will capture the stories of Your faithfulness to me and my family so future generations will know Your goodness. They will remember because I have left behind MEMORIALS.

It is important to pause and remember what God has done. What He has brought you to and brought you through. It is important to mark these milestones in ways that our children and their children can look back and see the faithfulness of God and have their faith built. What memorials do you need to construct to show God's goodness?

GOD'S GOODNESS APPEARS

*But when the goodness and loving kindness of God our
Savior appeared, He saved us, not because of works done
by us in righteousness, but according to His own mercy, by
the washing of regeneration and renewal of the Holy Spirit.*

TITUS 3:4-5, ESV

I name this day GOD'S GOODNESS APPEARS. Because of His mercy, because of His kindness, not because of anything I have done; God saved me.

He shows up in the darkest parts of my heart, the most broken places in my soul, and there He makes His home in me. There, He restores and heals. There, GOD'S GOODNESS APPEARS.

We know that faith without works is dead, but we also know that all our good deeds—all our righteousness—is as filthy rags. These ideas are hard to reconcile. Do our works matter or don't they? They do. They honor God and activate our faith, but they do not earn His grace or our salvation. His goodness alone provides this. How do you feel about this?

ADDICTED TO JOY

The world of the generous gets larger and larger;
the world of the stingy gets smaller and smaller.
The one who blesses others is abundantly blessed;
those who help others are helped.

PROVERBS 11:24-25, MSG

I name this day ADDICTED TO JOY. Giving is contagious. Generosity a game-changer. When thoughts of lack are replaced with abundance, the heavens open and supply increases. My world gets larger and larger and larger. The more I bless others, the more abundantly I am blessed. Joy, joy, and more joy ... I am ADDICTED TO JOY!

God loves a cheerful giver. The kingdom of God is often at odds with the ways of the world. The more we give, the more generous we are, the more blessed we become, the more we are enlarged and expanded. God's ways work! In what ways can you be generous today?

CENTERED IN GOD'S LOVE

*But you, dear friends, carefully build yourselves up in
this most holy faith by praying in the Holy Spirit, staying
right at the center of God's love, keeping your arms open
and outstretched, ready for the mercy of our Master,
Jesus Christ. This is the unending life, the real life!*

JUDE 1:20-21, MSG

I name this day CENTERED IN GOD'S LOVE. I build myself up in the faith by praying in the Spirit. This keeps me at the center of God's love. I worship the Creator with my arms open and outstretched. I recognize all that is around me teeming with God-life! I do not live a shadow life or make due with a faint copy. I live a real life, a live that is overflowing with abundance because I am CENTERED IN GOD'S LOVE.

How do you build yourself up in the faith? What does praying in the Spirit look like for you? Open your arms today and keep them outstretched. Ask God to place you in the center of His love.

FRESH WINESKINS

But new wine must be put into fresh wineskins.

LUKE 5:38, AMP

I name this day FRESH WINESKINS. I like the old things. They are mellow, familiar, and comfortable. But that is yesterday. Change comes regardless of whether I like it or not.

Therefore, today I prepare my heart to receive new wine. I look to the future with anticipation and not dread. Faithfully and with joy, I make ready for a new outpouring with FRESH WINESKINS.

Faith experiences that are meaningful tempt us to build a memorial, camp there, and want to freeze time. But God rarely does the same thing the same way twice. Trying to contain Him in an old mindset ends in folly. How can you prepare fresh wineskins to receive His new outpouring?

MEASURED WORDS

The more talk, the less truth;
the wise measure their words.

PROVERBS 10:19, MSG

I name this day MEASURED WORDS. From my heart springs my speech. My words are a constant flow of declaration, more powerful than I am aware. All day my words reveal my thoughts and decree my beliefs. The truth is that I am in agreement with whatever is falling out of my mouth. Because I know my speech charts my course, I take care to be intentional about my thoughts. I purpose in my heart to speak MEASURED WORDS.

If you listen between the lines, you will soon understand the measure of what is inside a person's heart. If they listen well to you, your heart will make itself known to them as well. Measure your words. What are they telling you about your beliefs?

A MATTER OF COURSE

So don't worry and don't keep saying, "What shall we eat,
what shall we drink, or what shall we wear?"
That is what pagans are always looking for;
your Heavenly Father knows that you need them all.
Set your heart on the kingdom and His goodness, and
all these things will come to you as a matter of course.

MATTHEW 6:31-33, PHILLIPS

I name this day A MATTER OF COURSE. I will keep the main things main. I will attend to my priorities in the right order, the right way, and for the right reasons. I will set my heart on God's kingdom and His goodness. All the other stuff has an expiration date anyway, so I will pay attention to the things which are eternal. I will seek first His kingdom, everything else will come as A MATTER OF COURSE.

Are you anxious? Do you worry about bills, clothes, social obligations? Your job, your family, your future? You are not alone. But God encourages us to set our hearts on His kingdom, to focus on His goodness, to seek Him first. His promise is that when we do, all those things we worry about get taken care of by Him. What a promise!

LIGHT TO LIVE BY

*Everything was created through Him; nothing—
not one thing—came into being without Him!
What came into existence was Life, and the Life
was Light to live by. The Life-Light blazed out of
the darkness; the darkness couldn't put it out.*

JOHN 1:3-5, MSG

I name this day LIGHT TO LIVE BY. Jesus came to earth fully man and fully the Son of God. He is my beacon. The light for my path. The illuminator of my soul.

Jesus if Life-Light, dispelling the darkness in my heart. He reveals the stuff I try to keep hidden. His light is warm and kind and envelops me in a blanket of glory. Jesus is my LIGHT TO LIVE BY.

Merry Christmas! The Light of the World has come! Hosanna in the highest! Celebrate the coming of Christ today. Let every light you see— candles, lamps, holiday lights—let each one of them herald His coming and remind you that He illuminates you. Amen.

PUBLISH HIS GLORY

Sing to God, everyone and everything!
Get out His salvation news every day!
Publish His glory among the godless nations,
His wonders to all races and religions. And why?
Because God is great—well worth praising!

1 CHRONICLES 16:24, MSG

I name this day PUBLISH HIS GLORY. The cultural climate can make us shy, unwilling to share our experiences of faith for fear of creating offense or being misunderstood. But God's goodness is present all around. His acts are amazing, and our testimony helps us overcome. So today, with kindness, with tact, grace, and unbridled love, let's tell everyone—PUBLISH HIS GLORY!

PUBLISH: to make widely known, to make
public announcement of.

Telling people about the goodness of God and salvation that comes through His Son, Jesus, is not scary. When God has changed your life and made you reborn, it is the most natural thing in the world to do. What holds you back from sharing about Jesus? Who could you share Him with today?

WORKMANSHIP

*For we are His workmanship, created in Christ
Jesus unto good works, which God hath before
ordained that we should walk in them.*

EPHESIANS 2:10, KJV

I name this day WORKMANSHIP. I am God's poem, His masterpiece. I was finely crafted by His loving hand, with purpose, for His pleasure. This greatness is in me. This purpose calls to me, and I will rise to it. I will answer it with joy and a glad heart. What a wonder—I am God's WORKMANSHIP!

Have you ever considered that you are God's work of art? He has lovingly designed you for good works. Before you were in your mother's womb, He crafted your personality, temperament, and giftings. Pause today and think about yourself as a masterpiece. Study yourself and notice God's glory shining through you.

DARE TO HOPE

Yet I still dare to hope when I remember this:
the faithful love of the Lord never ends!
His mercies never cease.

LAMENTATIONS 3:21-22, NLT

I name this day DARE TO HOPE. Each day brings new mercies, and with them comes the opportunity for a fresh start. It is never too late to begin anew.

I will make great choices today. I will be grateful. I will be kind. I decree newness and fulfilled promises. I move ahead with inspired intentionality. I DARE TO HOPE.

He is the God of miracles! His supernatural power is still active in the earth today. It is easy to become jaded because of the faithlessness of men, but cynicism is toxic to faith. Approach God with awe today and let Him stir the miraculous in your soul.

DECEMBER 29

RUN WITH ENDURANCE

*You need the strength of endurance to reveal the poetry
of God's will and then you receive the promise in full.*

HEBREWS 10:36, TPT

I name this day RUN WITH ENDURANCE. Life is a marathon, not a sprint. I have to pace myself, employ strategy, discipline, training, support, and make sure I rest!

The strength of endurance reveals the poetry of God's will. Cadence, rhythm, timing. He causes my seasons to rhyme. As I run my race, the promises unfold. Promise fulfilled, promises yet to come. This builds my confidence, and that confidence helps me forge ahead where no one else has yet been. Wherever my path leads, I will run well. However long God grants me, I will RUN WITH ENDURANCE.

What race has been set before you? As the year is drawing to a close, it is a good time to pause and reflect on where you began in January, and to where you have come now. What went well? What went wrong? What remains that you will keep pursuing in the days ahead? Find your lane and run with endurance.

DECEMBER 30

INTENTIONALITY

God will continually revitalize you, implanting
within you the passion to do what pleases Him.

PHILIPPIANS 2:13, TPT

I name this day INTENTIONALITY. I live with purpose, on purpose.

I guard my thoughts. I choose my words and actions carefully. I shape the atmosphere around me. I make choices consciously that push me in the direction I desire for a hopeful, positive, possible future. I ask God for wisdom, and He constantly revitalizes me. He gives me passion—the fuel I need to do what pleases Him—so I can walk with INTENTIONALITY.

> *INTENTIONALITY: a quality of thoughts, beliefs,*
> *hopes, and desires that direct you with purpose*
> *toward the object or state of your intention.*
> *"If the outcome you want is a nail driven into a*
> *board, then intention is the fully aligned*
> *force behind the hammer."*

Do you live with purpose? Do you live on purpose or do you allow your days to unfold and bring you along in their wake? We have the privilege of choice. The honor to decide the direction of our focus and the passionate pursuit of our purpose. How can you be more intentional today?

381

FINISH WELL

*But my life is worth nothing to me unless I use
it for finishing the work assigned me by the
Lord Jesus—the work of telling others the Good
News about the wonderful grace of God.*

ACTS 20:24, NLT

I name this day FINISH WELL. I will run my race with intention, knowing every step I take is on purpose, with a specific direction.

I decree a finisher's anointing and I purpose in my heart that what I begin I will complete. Just as He who began a good work in me is faithful to complete it. I will do greater works through Christ who strengthens me. I will testify of His goodness. With a heart of purpose, I will FINISH WELL.

It is the last day of the year. Tomorrow you begin a new chapter with a fresh start. As you ponder the year ahead, determine that you will finish well. Step into the provision of a finisher's anointing and agree with God to finish what you start.

Death and life are in the power of the tongue ...

PROVERBS 18:21a, NKJV

You will also declare a thing,
And it will be established for you;
So light will shine on your ways.

JOB 22:28, NKJV

I NAME THIS DAY

_____

_____

_____

_____

_____

_____

_____

_____

_____

_____

_____

_____

FOR MORE BOOKS, COURSES,
AND OTHER RESOURCES

WWW.WENDYKWALTERS.COM

Made in United States
Orlando, FL
23 January 2022

13962846R00217